Antalya Turkey Travel Guide.

Tourism

Author
Daniel Anderson

Copyright Policy

Information-Source This Title is protected by Copyright Policy, any intention to reproduce, distribute and sales of this Title without the permission from the Title owner is strictly prohibited. Please when purchasing this Title, make sure that you obtain the necessary reference related to the purchase such as purchasing receipt. In accordance with this term, you are permitted to have access to this Title. Thanks for understanding and cooperation.

All-right reserved Information-Sourve
Copyright 2021..

Published
By
Information-Source.
16192 Coastal Highway Lewes,
DE 19958. USA.
.

Table of Content

ABOUT ANTALYA. 1

INTRODUCTION 1
THE HISTORY 5
ANTALYA TOURISM 10
TRAVEL GUIDE 51

Guide to Antalya 55
   Antalya Orientation 55
   Antalya Weather and Climate 58
   Antalya Airport Guide 62
      Airport Hotels and Accommodation 68
      History Overview 70
      Airlines, Terminals and Facilities 72
      Airport Transportation 77
      Airport Climate and Weather 81
   City Information 83
   Sightseeing in Antalya 89
   Family trip with kids 95
   Unusual weekend 99
   Culture: sights to visit 104
   Attractions & nightlife 111
      Antalya Other Attractions 117
         Archaeological Museum in Antalya 117
         Atatürk's House Museum in Antalya 134
         Broken Minaret in Antalya 140
         City Walls of Antalya 144
         Hadrian's Gate in Antalya 149
         Hıdırlık Tower in Antalya 156
   Planning a Trip in Antalya 159
      Fast Facts in Antalya 167
   Cuisine & restaurants 170
   Traditions & lifestyle 176
   Where to stay? 183
      Extraordinary hotels 183
      Stylish design-hotels 187
      Hotels with history 191
      Luxury accommodation 196

Romantic hotel 200
Shopping in Antalya 204
Tips for tourists 209

About Antalya.
Introduction

The biggest attraction of Antalya is its exquisite natural beauty. Antalya gives you the best of Mediterranean climate with long summers, pleasant winters and lots of sunshine. So enjoy your summer travel to the fullest at this perfect holiday destination. The natural elegance of Antalya is well complemented by its plenteous historic past.

The City Walls and the Hadrian Gate are historical remnants of the rich Roman style. These structures are hot favorites of tourists.

Kaleici is the heart of Antalya and has been the nerve centre of the city from its historic past. Consequently, it's a showcase of its vibrant archeological wealth. The spot has also been restored recently to fit in modern hotels, malls, restaurants and entertainment joints. The renovations bagged the biggest prize in tourism. So why not spend that vacation in the best destination.

The Antalya Museum is one of the most renowned archeological museums of the world. Other spots of interest are the Kesik Minaret of the Byzantine era, the Yivli Minaret of the Seljuks, the Karatay Medresesi, Hidirilk Tower, Ahi Yusuf Mescidi, Iskele Mosque, Murat Pasa Mosque, Tekeli Mehmet Pasa Mosque and Balibey Mosque. There are many Hans or inns in the typical Seljuk and Ottoman fashion.

Antalya also forms a pivotal junction for your travel to other spots of interest in Turkey. The popular options are the historically rich locations of Termessos, Perge, Sillyon, Aspendos, Pamukkale and Cappadocia.

Antalya, Turkey's principal holiday resort in the Mediterranean region (ancient Pamphylia), is an attractive city with shady palm-lined boulevards, a prize-winning marina on the Mediterranean. In the picturesque old quarter, Kaleici, narrow winding streets and old wooden houses abut the ancient city walls. Lately, many foreigners have bought (and continue to buy) property in and around Antalya for their holidays or for the retirement. It became a popular area especially for the German and Russian nationals. During the winter months its population is around 2,5 million, but in the summer times it doubles!

fluted minaret in AntalyaSince its founding in the second century BC by Attalus II, a king of Pergamon, who named the city Attaleai after himself, Antalya has been continuously inhabited. The Romans, the Byzantines and the Seljuks in turn occupied the city before it came under Ottoman rule. The elegant fluted minaret of the Yivli Minareli Mosque in the center of the city built by the Seljuk sultan Alaeddin Keykubad I in the 13th century has become the Antalya's symbol. The Karatay Medrese (theological college) in the Kaleici district, from the same period, exemplifies the best of Seljuk stone carvings. The two most important Ottoman mosques in the city are the 16th century Murat Pasa Mosque, remarkable for its tile decoration, the 18th century Tekeli Mehmet Pasa Mosque. Neighboring the marina, the attractive late 19th century Iskele Mosque is built of cut stone and set on four pillars over a natural spring. The Hidirlik Kulesi (tower) was probably originally constructed as a lighthouse in the second century. Today a church, the Kesik Minaret Mosque attests to the city's long history in its succession of Roman, Byzantine, Seljuk and Ottoman renovations. When Emperor Hadrian visited Antalya in 130 AD a beautifully decorated three arched gate was built into the city walls in his honor.

Near the marina the two towers flanking the gate and other sections of the walls still stand. The clock tower in Kalekapisi Square was also part of the old city's fortifications.

The History

Antalya Province Is The Most Important And The Largest Tourism City In The South Of Turkey. It Is Located In The West Of The Mediterranean Region. There Are Taurus Mountains On The Back Of Antalya. Antalya Province Has Become The Sixth Largest Province Of Turkey By Growing Rapidly In The Field Of Tourism Since 1980. İt Is A Pretty City Economically Based On Trade, Agriculture And Tourism. From Past To Present, Antalya Has Hosted Many Famous Civilizations In The History. The Most Ancient Cities Such As Lycians, Pamphilians, Lydians, Byzantines, The Romans Seljuk And Ottomans Is All Located In Antalya Region. Most Of Turkey S Vegetable Production Is Made In Alanya, Kaş, Kalkan And Patra.

The Hittite State, Which Is One Of The Most Important Periods Of Antalya Province, Was

Established In The Middle Anatolia In The First Place, But Later Reached To Antalya. İt Is Mentioned In The Greek Mythology That Due To The Destruction Of The Hittite Empire, There Was Migration Of Akads To The Region.

In The Last Seljuk Period, Anatolia Went Under The Population Of Ilhanians After 1300 During The Anatolian Turkish Principalities And Antalya Began To Establish Tribes And Principalities In The Westends.

Karabıkıkoğlu Whose Name Has Been Mentioned In The Historical Sources And Rebellion In The Year Of 1511 Is More Known As Sahkulu Tekeli. He Was The Son Of Sheikh Hasan , The Caliph Of The Shah Ismail's Father And Came From The Village Of Kizilkaya.

The Year 1919 Is One Of The Darkest Years Of Turkish Nation. From The Soldiers Who Went To The World War I Only 1 In 3 Were Able To Return. Those Whom Returned Either With A Lost Their Leg Or Arm. Antalya And Its Surroundings Were Given To The Kingdom Of Italy With The Armistice Agreement Signed After The War. During These Periods, The Invaders Could Invade Any Part Of The Province Of Antalya As Wished, Freeing The Military Agencies And Destroying The Whole Place.

The Great Offensive Known As The Battle Of Dumplupinar Started On The 26th Of August With A Small Turkish Army. After The Army Captured Afyonkarahisar City, The News Spreaded To Antalya. Turks Started To Get Organized Happily And On The 30th Of August With The Victory Of Dumplupinar, The Greeks

Lost The Battle. On The Other Hand, They Gathered At Night In The Farms In Antalya. On September The 11th, The Victory Procession Was Held In Antalya And People Celebrated This Day With A Great Joy. The Societies And The Public Have Arranged Lantern Regiments At Night Until The Morning.

After October 29, 1923, Major Changes Occured In The City Of Antalya As In The Whole Of The Turkish State. Antalya, Which Was A Sanjak During The Ottoman Period, Became A Province Of Turkey During The Republican Period. Antalya Which Grown Gradually In 1923 Has Taken A Turn After The Proclamation Of The Republic And Begun To Grow With Rapid Migration. Since 1974, It Has Became The Most Developed Tourism City In Turkey.

Antalya Tourism

Antalya is a city that is difficult not to fall in love with. Its beauty enchanted ancient authors, explorers and travellers that visited the Ottoman Empire were stunned by its charms, and even the father of modern Turkey and the first president of the Turkish Republic, Mustafa Kemal Atatürk, expressed his fascination in Antalya in superlatives only. On the one hand, Antalya is currently a metropolis with the population of over a million inhabitants, but on the other hand - it is also increasingly popular tourist resort with beautiful beaches and luxury hotels. What's more, in the heart of the city there is a charming historical district, and the collections gathered in the local Archaeological Museum are among the most attractive in the whole of Turkey. What will Antalya be for you? Certainly, it is a city worth a visit and checking if it actually is "the most beautiful place on earth."

Frequently repeated and most well-known version of the history of Antalya states that the city was founded in the Hellenistic period, around 150 BCE, by Attalos II, king of Pergamon. The city was then called Attalia, reflecting its founder's name. Over time this word was distorted and now exists as Antalya. However, a recent archaeological discovery in the district Doğu Garajı can attest to the fact that the city was founded slightly earlier, in the 3rd century BCE. This version is not surprising at all, if one considers an extremely favourable location of Antalya, conducive to its development as a port city, and the prehistoric traces of human activity found in the nearby Karain cave.

One way or another, most certainly Attalos II served the city well, expanding it and appointing it the role of the main port of his kingdom. However, Antalya did not remain under the control of Pergamon for long. In 133 BCE, the last ruler of this state died, leaving his kingdom in his will to Rome. From this moment Antalya developed as an important Roman city, attracting many traders and travellers. The most famous personality who visited it at the beginning of the first millennium CE was St. Paul of Tarsus. His journey from the northern land known as Pisidia to the port of Antalya is now commemorated by the recently mapped walking trail.

In the Byzantine period Antalya, a city with a rank of a bishopric, many churches were erected. Among these buildings, the one worth mentioning is the church dedicated to the Virgin Mary, in later times converted into a mosque, and now known as the Broken Minaret. It is located in the historic district, Kaleiçi, towering above the port from Roman times. From the 7th century, Antalya was the target of Arab invasions and, simultaneously, gained more strategic importance as the military outpost, guarding the southern coast of Asia Minor. In those days the city was the capital of the Byzantine military district (i.e. theme), known as the Cibyrrhaeots.

After the period of Arab raids a new threat started to loom over the lands of Asia Minor in the form of Seljuk Turks that arrived from the east and gradually conquered this land. At the end of the 11th century Antalya was captured by the Seljuk troops, but soon they were forced to withdraw. Byzantine control over the city was restored thanks to the political conditions created by the First Crusade. However, in 1118 Antalya was surrounded by areas under the control of local Seljuk warlords. The only connection it had with the Byzantine territories was by sea routes. Finally, at the beginning of the 13th century, the city was conquered by the Turks.

After sacking and occupation of Constantinople by the Fourth Crusade, Antalya was captured for a short period by the Italians but soon returned to the Seljuks. They made the city the capital of Teke beylik (a small ancestral kingdom). In the second half of the 14th century Peter I of Cyprus, the Christian king of Cyprus and titular king of Jerusalem he exercised control over Antalya for 12 years. The appearance of the city in the 14th century was described by the famous Arab traveller Ibn Battuta. He marvelled at Adalia, as the city was then known under this name, especially its beautiful location with a decent organisation and multicultural character.

Antalya was incorporated into the Ottoman Empire in 1423 by Sultan Murad II. From the 15th century to the early 20th century, the city retained its multiethnic character. There were, among others, four Greek neighbourhoods in Antalya. In the second half of the 17th century, according to the Turkish traveller Evliya Çelebi, there were three thousand houses in the city, and its area exceeded the ancient walls.

From the end of World War I until 1923 Antalya was occupied by the Italian troops. The city had then 30,000 residents. Following the restoration of control over Antalya by the Turkish Republic, its ethnic composition underwent a massive transformation. The Greek population that lived here for many centuries was resettled to Greece, and its place was taken by the Turks from the Balkans and the Caucasus. Until the early 70th of the 20th century, the town was actually a farming and fishing village. Since then, however, Antalya has completely changed, partially due to the tourism boom. Currently, with over 1 million inhabitants, Antalya is one of the largest and most modern Turkish metropolitan areas.

The most important Seljuk and Ottoman monuments in Antalya are located in Kaleiçi and its immediate vicinity. If you have just a few hours in the city, you can spend time just in this area, walking along its narrow streets, visiting historic mosques and watching the mighty ramparts with the magnificent Hadrian's Gate. Pay special attention to the most important symbol of the city - the Fluted Minaret (tr. *Yivli Minare*), as well as to the ruins of a building known as the Broken Minaret (tr. *Kesik Minare*) and Hıdırlık Tower. Visit a nearby Karaalioğlu Park and the Roman harbour at the foot of Kaleiçi.

Those interested in ancient history should visit the Archaeological Museum, located on the western side of Antalya. This museum is one of the finest of its kind in Turkey, and you can spend many hours admiring the exhibits in its collections. There are indeed more museums in Antalya, among which worth mentioning are: Atatürk House (tr. *Atatürk Evi ve Müzesi*), the Ethnographic Museum within the Fluted Minaret Mosque complex and a private museum known as Suna-İnan Kıraç Kaleiçi Müzesi.

Local points of interest also include Toy Museum (tr. *Oyuncak Muzesi*), located near the historic harbour and the Museum of Furnaces (tr. *Soba Müzesi*). The latter, the only one of its kind in the country, has in its collections many specimens of ovens and furnaces, including the models imported from Italy and France, beautifully decorated with ceramic tiles. The facility is housed in a cylindrical structure on Şht. Binbaşı Cengiz Toytunç street (36.888370, 30.708172), north of Kaleiçi, just off the bazaar area. The museum is open daily, except Mondays, between 9:30 am and 6:30 pm, and the normal admission ticket costs 6 TL.

The latest addition to Antalya museum network is the Museum of Cinema (tr. *Behlül Dal Sinema Müzesi*), opened in July 2013. Unfortunately, despite a promising idea and close links Antalya has with the art of film, a visit to the museum can bring great disappointment - a modest collection of equipment and film posters does not encourage its exploration. If you want to check for yourself whether the museum creators had done a good job this venue is located in a restored Greek house, near Karaalioğlu Park and Atatürk House, at 1305 Sokak Street (36.881005, 30.709330). The museum is closed on Mondays and can be visited from 9:30 am to 12:30 and from 1:30 pm to 6:30 pm. The admission cost is 6 TL.

The raiders of historical curiosities in Antalya should find modest remains of a Roman bridge Arapsu (36.880906, 30.659346), located at the foot of the mound associated with the Greek colony of Olbia. This partially sunken bridge is located between 5M Migros shopping centre and

Antalya Aquarium water park, in the western side of the city. In addition, just by the D650 route, leading from Antalya to the north-west, several Seljuk-period tombs (called türbe) are still standing.

The most important statues in the city are: the equestrian statue of Mustafa Kemal Atatürk standing on the Square of the Republic (36.886685, 30.703265) and a monument to the city's founder, the king of Pergamon Attalos II (36.887227, 30.705488), standing in front of the Clock Tower. In the city centre, there are numerous modern sculptures depicting many characters, including - a tea carrier, a janitor and children at play. A picturesque alley, where tourists flock to take some photos, is the 2. İnönü Sokak known as Umbrella Street because it is shaded by a lot of multi-colored umbrellas (36.886833, 30.707333).

Antalya is a convenient starting point for many excursions to the ancient cities of Perge, Termessos, Sillyon and Aspendos as well as to the Karain Cave. The famous Lycian Way hiking trail through the Taurus mountains begins in Antalya and finishes in Fethiye.

Moreover, in the vicinity of Antalya starts St. Paul hiking trail. It is a marked trail leading from Perge to Yalvaç, north-east of Lake Eğirdir. The second branch of the trail begins in Aspendos and connects with the first one in Adad - the desolate ruins of the Roman city. The total length of the route is about 500 km. The trail partly follows in the footsteps of the Apostle Paul on his first missionary journey through Asia Minor.

The centre of the city

Antalya is located on the Mediterranean coast, on the deep Gulf of Antalya (tr. *Antalya Körfezi*). The city is situated in a place where the conventional border runs between the historic lands: Lycia to the east and Pamphilia to the west. To the north of Antalya, in the depths of the Anatolian peninsula, lies a land called Pisidia.

At the heart of the city, there is its oldest part known as Kaleiçi district, perched above the historic harbour, remembering the Roman period. At Kaleiçi the main thoroughfares of the city converge. To the north of Kaleiçi stretches a commercial district of the city, whose main axis is transformed into a pedestrian Kazım Özalp street. It houses a variety of shops and the historic covered bazaar.

To the west of Kaleiçi runs in an arc of Atatürk street, leading along the historic ramparts, including the famous Hadrian's Gate. At the southern end of the street stands the Municipal Office (tr. *Antalya Büyükşehir Belediyesi*), located on the border of a magnificent Karaalioğlu park. In the same area, there is a museum known as Atatürk House (tr. *Atatürk Evi ve Müzesi*).

Going further south after 3 km you can reach the beach district of Lara, extending over a distance of 12 km along the sea coast. It is the most famous cluster of resort hotels in the city. In this district, there is an exhibition area called Sandland where every year an exhibition of sand sculptures in held, and a picturesque Lower Düden Waterfall, falling from a high cliff into the sea.

On the northern side of Kaleiçi, the Street of the Republic (tr. *Cumhuriyet Caddesi*) passes further to the west where it takes the name Konyaaltı. At the beginning of this street, there is the Square of the Republic (tr. *Cumhuriyet Meydanı*), decorated by a magnificent monument erected to the first president of Turkey - Mustafa Kemal Atatürk. Konyaaltı Street leads towards the western districts of the city and the Konyaaltı beach. Along this thoroughfare, on the coastal side, there are many green areas and city parks.

If you go west 2.5 km from the Clock Tower standing on the border of Kaleiçi district, you will reach the Archaeological Museum. About 1.5 km further to the west there is an important intersection with the national road D400, with Migros shopping centre nearby. If, from this point, you will continue to the south-west, after

1 km you will reach the entertainment area, where there the famous marine park Aquarium, a miniature park called Minicity, and a dolphinarium are located. In the direction of the coast stretches Konyaaltı Beach, where many luxury hotels are situated.

Antalya is located on an important national route D400, which runs along the southern coast of Turkey, from the town of Datça located in the west to Adana far in the east. Further on, the same route runs through the south-eastern Anatolia to the border with Iran. For those visiting the Turkish Riviera route D400 is the main communication route, linking Antalya in the west of the holiday resorts, including - Side and Alanya, in the east. Taking this route from Antalya to the west you can reach the coast of

Lycia, including such towns as Kemer, Fethiye and Demre.

On the D400 road, just to the east from the centre of Antalya, there is the most important airport in the region called Antalya Havalimanı. A little further east, in the town of Aksu, the road D685 to Isparta in the Lake Region branches off the route D400. On this route, there is Kurşunlu Waterfall, which is a frequent target of local excursions. In the village of Aksu lie the ruins of the famous ancient city of Perge.

The most important transportation junction is located to the north-west of the centre of Antalya. This a is huge roundabout where the route D400 turns south to Lycia, and the road D650 leads north, through Burdur and Afyonkarahisar to the Black Sea coast. On the road D650, 3 km further north, lies a huge bus terminal of Antalya (tr. *Antalya Otogarı*). It is located just 6 km from the historical centre of Antalya.

About 10 km further to the north the route to Burdur forks off, and its left branch (road D350) runs north-west to the town of Korkuteli and continues to Denizli. It is the road taken by coaches carrying tourists to the famous Pamukkale. Not far from Antalya you can turn left from this road, to get to the ruins of the ancient Termessos, or to the right - to Karain cave that was inhabited in prehistoric times.

In the case of the very centre of Antalya or Kaleiçi district and the adjoining area of the bazaar and the Karaalioğlu, the easiest and most convenient way is to explore it on foot. The distances here are not large, and the area is largely a pedestrian zone with very limited access for cars.

The access to more remote districts of the city as well as from the airport and the bus terminal is easy because of a well-organized public transport system. Travellers have a choice of bus and tram networks, and, additionally, there are numerous minibuses (called dolmuş in Turkey). For individuals with a larger budget city taxis wait in various areas of the city.

In Antalya, there are two tram lines. The first of them, that has been in operation for many years, is traditional tramway, known as Nostalgic Tram or *Nostalji Tramvay*. Its route goes from the western part of town, from the Konyaaltı beach and the Archaeological Museum to the historical centre, where it stops at the main gates leading to the Kaleiçi district, and further south, along the Karaalioğlu Park to Lara beach.

Since along almost the entire route of this line there is only one track only two trams travel it, passing each other in the vicinity of Kalekapısı gate, where a double track is prepared for this purpose. Trams depart every half hour from the terminal, and the ride along the entire route, divided into ten stops, takes less than half an hour. Nostalji Tramvay runs daily from 7 am to 9 pm.

The second tram line in Antalya is actually a modern railway system, called AntRay. It runs from the north-west of the city, from the district of Fatih, through the bus terminal and the city centre to the south-eastern districts. This line provides the most convenient access from the bus terminal to the heart of the city (İsmetpaşa tram stop). AntRay has, at present, 16 stops and it runs every 15 minutes. Its schedule changes on Sundays and holidays, but essentially the tram can be used from 6 am to 11 pm.

Unfortunately, these two tram lines do not have a transit point, which would enable a quick change of the route. Two stops, located closest to each other are situated in the centre of Antalya. Here İsmetpaşa stop (for AntRay) and Kalekapısı stop (for Nostalji Tramvay) are situated less than 300 meters away.

A single ride tram ticket price for both lines is 1.75 TL. In the case of AntRay, there are also cards with QR code, enabling three rides. The code is scanned each time you enter the tram platform. Tickets can be purchased at retail outlets at tram stops, but they usually close around 7 pm, so if you plan to travel later in the evening, you might want to obtain tickets in advance.

Almost any place in Antalya that cannot be reached by trams is accessible by a network of bus and minibus connections. In addition to the numbers of individual lines, there are extremely helpful letters visible on many buses, which denote the end stop for the particular course. For example, the letter A represents Aksu city on the east side of Antalya, K - Konyaaltı Beach and L - Lara Beach. The airport is connected to the bus terminal by the lines 600 and 202 (through the centre of the city).

Taxi stands can be found in many parts of the city, and the most popular travel destinations have predetermined prices listed on the notice boards. From midnight to 6 am the fares increase by 50%. Before taking a taxi you should enquire about the fee. The ride from the center to the airport during the day should cost about 35-40 TL, and to the bus terminal - 25-30 TL.

In Antalya, as in other Turkish cities with an airport nearby, there are shuttle buses, referred to as Havaş. However, in Antalya, their travel route bypasses the strict historical city centre, leading from Route D400, to the bus terminal to the west of the city and 5M Migros shopping centre. Buses run every hour from early morning until 10 pm, and their departure times from the airport are synchronised with the arrivals of domestic flights. The price of one ride is 10 TL.

Finding a restaurant in Antalya is not difficult, as in the city centre they are situated practically everywhere. Moreover, in contrast to the situation in Alanya, where a lot of venues are geared solely to draw money from the foreigners unfamiliar with the culinary realities of Turkey, almost all restaurants in Antalya keep a high level for a decent price.

In Kaleiçi districts restaurants and bars are literally at every step. Some of them, like Vanilla on Zafer street No. 13 or Seraser Restaurant that belongs to Tuvana Hotel serve international dishes. Others, including Sim on Kaledibi Street No. 7 and Gül on Kocatepe street No. 1 specialise in traditional Turkish cuisine.

In search of cheaper restaurants head to the so-called Dönerciler Çarşısı or covered bazaar, located on the north-eastern side of Kaleiçi, on Atatürk street. In this area there are several restaurants, serving mainly the local clientele, and though they lack the particular charm of the historic district, the dishes they serve are tasty and reasonably priced. If you feel up to the challenge go to Şampiyon Kokoreç restaurant, which specialises in a dish called *kokoreç*, prepared from lamb intestines. You can also choose tasty stuffed clams (tr. *midye dolma*).

If you are after bars and nightclubs, you can check the Kaleiçiarea, where there are many pubs and wine bars, located in gardens surrounded by high walls for privacy. However, the nightlife center of Antalya is situated in the western district of Konyaaltı beach, where one can find discos, clubs and bars with a wide selection of alcoholic drinks.

As the capital of the province, Antalya has the largest and best-stocked supermarkets and shopping malls in the region. If you are not interested in shopping on the traditional bazaar or in shops offering cheap imitations of famous brands that are abundant in all resorts on the

Turkish Riviera, go directly to Antalya and its upmarket shopping options.

The largest mall in the city is TerraCity (36.852649, 30.756202), located in the Lara district, east of the centre. It is open daily from 10 am to 10 pm. The most important Turkish clothing companies, as well as many foreign brands, have their shops there. Of course, there are also drugstores, jewellers, interior decoration shops, electronics shops and restaurants. Please note that the prices in the shops of some companies are higher than their smaller branches in other districts of the city or, for example, in Alanya - a cost that you have to pay for a wider selection and a touch of luxury.

Among the other shopping centres in Antalya, it is worth mentioning 5M Migros (36.883399, 30.658131) with about 130 different shops, located in Muratpaşa district, near the Antalya Aquarium and miniature park. To the north of the historic city centre, in the district of Kepez, there is Özdilek shopping centre (36.910522, 30.677807), where you will find 100 shops, 20 restaurants, a hypermarket and a cinema.

In search of bargain prices for designer clothing visit Deepo Outlet Center (36.920508, 30.786021), the largest of its kind in the Mediterranean region of Turkey. It is located east of the city centre, close to the international airport and the road leading in the direction of Manavgat and Alanya.

The largest bazaar in Antalya is conveniently located just off Kaleiçi, along Kazım Özalp Caddesi street (36.888776, 30.704983). The distinctive landmark is enabling it to find it is a monument to the founder of the city, Attalos II.

The part of this area is a historic covered bazaar, İki Kapılar Hanı, built in the 15th century.

Other services

The tourist information office operates in the Republic Square (tr. *Cumhuriyet Meydanı*), just west of the Fluted Minaret (36.886741, 30.704166).

A self-service launderette operates in Kaleiçi, on Hıdırlık street No. 10 (36.883335, 30.705505). There you do your laundry for a few liras and, at an additional cost, dry the entire batch.

The post office branches nearest to the old town are located on 1261 Sokak (36.886769, 30.710589) and 1267 Sokak (36.887227, 30.708907), north-west of Kaleiçi.

The easiest way to find banks and ATMs is to walk along the Street of the Republic (tr.

Cumhuriyet Caddesi) and one of its extensions to the east i.e. Ali Cetinkaya street.

By plane: Antalya Airport (tr. *Antalya Havalimanı*) is one of the most important airports in Turkey from a tourist point of view, being for many vacationers the gateway to summer holidays and the first place they see in the country. The airport was built in 1960, but the real boom of tourism on the Turkish Riviera is closely linked to its expansion in the 90s of the 20th century. In 2013, the airport handled 21.5 million passengers from abroad. The airport is located to the east of the centre of Antalya and consists of two international and one domestic terminal.

The most prominent airlines that operate from Antalya Airport are: AnadoluJet, Turkish Airlines, Corendon Airlines, Freebird Airlines, Pegasus

Airlines and SunExpress. The airport is heavily busy during the summer season, when millions of holidaymakers arrive by charter flights to the Turkish Riviera. Off-season, the number of connections drops significantly, but throughout the year there are maintained connections to many European cities, including several airports in Germany.

From Antalya Airport you can also fly to several other cities in Turkey. Frequently held flights include these to Istanbul (1 hour and 15 minutes, from 60 TL), both to Atatürk and Sabiha Gökçen airports. In addition, at least once a day, there are direct flights to Turkey's capital city - Ankara (1 hour, 70 TL), Adana in the east of the country, Izmir - an important port on the Aegean Sea and Samsun - the largest city on the Black Sea coast. To fly to other Turkish airports, you need to buy a connecting flight, with a stopover in Istanbul or Ankara.

By coach: a huge bus terminal of Antalya is located on the north-western side of the city. Both long-distance coaches and local services depart from it to nearby towns such as Serik, Manavgat, Alanya and Fethiye. There are two terminals actually - interurban (tr. *Şehirler Arası Terminalı*) for long-distance routes and local for nearby locations (tr. *İlçeler İlçeler Terminali*).

Keep in mind that in Turkey there are many bus companies, so tickets should be bought directly from such an operator. After entering the station just give the name of your destination, and you will be brought to the proper point of ticket sales.

Coaches go from Antalya to most of the cities in Turkey. The most important long-distance routes are: Istanbul (12 hours, 60 TL), Ankara (8 hours, 45 TL), Adana (10-12 hours, from 55 TL), Denizli - near Pamukkale (4-5 hours, from 35 TL), Göreme in Cappadocia (10 hours, 50 TL), Konya (6 hours, 30 TL), Izmir (8 hours, 45 TL) and Samsun (16 hours, 65 TL).

The most significant local connection is the one from Antalya to Alanya (2-3 hours, 20 TL), through Manavgat (a transfer point to Side, 1.5 hours and 15 TL) and Fethiye. If you are going to Fethiye, bear in mind that there are two routes for the coaches - a short, inland one (4 hours, 20 TL) and a longer, coastal one (7-8 hours, 25 TL).

By car: Antalya is a major transportation hub in southern Turkey. Several important roads cross near the city. Of these the most important one is the national road D400, running from the west to far east of the country. It is the road taken by most of the holidaymakers, heading to holiday resorts near Side and Alanya. The same route can take you to Adana further in the east and continue until the border with Iran or if you go to the west - to the towns on the Lycian coast. The distance from Antalya to Alanya is 135 km and 430 km to Adana. Travelling to Fethiye, you can select a scenic route along the Mediterranean coast, with a length of 300 km, but the journey is painfully slow. The advantage of choosing this option is passing through important historical cities of Lycia and beautiful scenery along the way. If you are in a hurry to get to the west, the better choice is the inland route D350, with the length of 200 km.

D350 route mentioned above is a part of the European road E87, which runs through Denizli (220 km) and Izmir (460 km) to Çanakkale (760 km). After the ferry crossing to Europe, the travellers leave the territory of Turkey by this route near the city of Edirne, going to Greece or Bulgaria.

In the northern direction, there are two parallel roads from Antalya: D650 to Burdur (120 km) in the Lake District and further on to the Black Sea coast (640 km) and D685 to Isparta (130 km). Antalya is connected with the central part of the country via the D695 route, veering off the coast in the town of Manavgat and leading to Konya (340 km).

Most of the people arriving in Antalya come there as part of the holiday packages purchased at travel agencies. Most likely they will be accommodated in one of two beach districts of the city - located at Lara Beach in the east or Konyaaltı Beach in the west. The hotels situated there are actually huge recreation centres, considered the most luxurious in the region of the Turkish Riviera, and thus - usually more expensive than hotels located in Side and Alanya.

However, if you arrive in Antalya on your own, you have a much wider choice of accommodation options. Of course, you can use the above mentioned holiday centers. However, the detailed analysis of their price lists for individual tourists frequently leads to the conclusion that it is significantly cheaper to buy a package holiday from a travel agent. You must also remember that the best of these hotels are booked through a travel agent well in advance and finding a free room in summer may not be possible.

Independent travellers frequently stop in Antalya in Kaleiçi district, where there are plenty of hotels and guesthouses of various standards. In all of the following hotels and guesthouses breakfast is included in the price.

Important note: people accustomed to using online booking services can be very surprised when looking for accommodation in Turkey. Firstly, many hotels and guest houses are not present in these services at all. Secondly, and most importantly, in contrast to the hotels from Western Europe, it often happens that the rates in the Turkish hotels are higher for booking online! Take a look at the available options, check whether the hotel has available rooms, then without reserving it go to the place, and then find out about prices and conditions. In many cases, the price proposed directly will be significantly lower, even by a half of the total cost.

The best boutique hotels in Kaleiçi district, offering a comfortable and memorable experience for visitors on a bigger budget, are:

- ✓ Tuvana Hotel - located on Karanlık street No. 18, this is one of the best hotels all over the Mediterranean coast of Turkey. The complex consists of six restored houses from the Ottoman era, and in the rooms, in addition to elegant decoration, all modern facilities are awaiting the travellers. A nice addition is a swimming pool for guests and highly praised Seraser Restaurant. Prices are high - an overnight stay in a double room costs from 330 TL up.

- ✓ Mediterra Art Hotel - Zafer Street No. 5, offers accommodation in a former Greek taverna, and guests have access to a swimming pool in the garden and a small art gallery. Prices are slightly lower - double room can be rented from 250 TL per day.

- ✓ Otantik Hotel - located on Hesapçi street No. 14. It is another hotel decorated in Ottoman style, with tastefully, but basically furnished rooms. An on-site restaurant has a fireplace and a well-stocked wine cellar. Accommodation for two people costs from 160 TL, but you can also rent a spacious apartment for 300 TL.

In Kaleiçi district there are also many cheap guesthouses, among which you should consider stopping at the following locations:

- ✓ White Garden Pansiyon - on Hesapçı Geçidi street No. 9. It offers simple and clean rooms, a swimming pool for guests and a tasty breakfast. The guest house has a private parking. Accommodation in a double room costs from 60 TL.

- ✓ Sabah Pansiyon - located on Hesapçı street No. 60. This pension offers both a bed in a dorm (25 TL), and simply furnished rooms with a private bathroom (55 TL) and without a bathroom (45 TL). People expecting a higher standard can rent spacious apartments for 200 TL.

- ✓ Mavi & Ani Pansiyon - at Tabakhane Sokak No 26. Another guest house decorated in Ottoman style, with the public areas decorated with antique furniture. The guests are offered rooms in Turkish and

European styles. The hotel has a swimming pool and private parking. Double room costs from 120 TL.

It is worth remembering that Kaleiçi district is a pedestrianised zone, not available for cars, that must be left on paid parking lots located on its outskirts. If you do not want to part with your vehicle, then you can consider stopping in hotels and guesthouses located in the centre of Antalya, but outside the historic district. Among these options we particularly recommend:

- ✓ Anadolu Pansiyon - located at the dead end of 1311 Sokak No 18, next to Karaalioğlu Park The advantage of this B&B are simply furnished but spacious rooms, private parking and a quiet environment. It is also difficult to resist the fresh breakfast prepared by the hostess. Double room costs

100 TL, and the guest house also has a large family room for 140 TL.

- ✓ Best Western Plus Khan Hotel - located along Kazim Özalp street No. 55, practically in the largest bazaar in Antalya. It offers free parking places, a terrace with a swimming pool and views of the city, and spacious rooms with balconies. Double rooms cost from 150 TL up.

- ✓ Metur Design Hotel - located on 1311 Sokak No. 18, the hotel is about 600 meters away from Kaleiçi and enjoys enthusiastic reviews from its guests. Unlike many hotels in the city, the rooms in this hotel are decorated in a modern style, and guests have a sizable swimming pool with sun loungers and a restaurant at their disposal. Prices for a double room start from 110 TL.

- ✓ Ramada Plaza Antalya - Fevzi Çakmak Street No. 22, is a great hotel, just off the sea coast, while less than 1 km from the historic Antalya district. There is a spa, three restaurants and a parking lot waiting for the guests. For a double room, you need to pay at least 170 TL, and it is possible to upgrade to all-inclusive option for a significant charge.

Travel Guide

The westerly region of Turkey's Mediterranean coastline is especially popular and sandy beaches around Antalya and the Konyaalti Bay are in abundance. With a particularly diverse landscape, it is actually quite feasible to enjoy a morning swim, and then head to the Taurus Mountains for a spot of skiing in the afternoon at the neighbouring resort of Davras.

Antalya's historical Old Town area known as the Kaleici offers beautiful harbour views and is surrounded by medieval fortified walls, which date back before both the Roman and Byzantine periods and have been restored many times. Currently the fasted-growing city in Turkey, Antalya enjoys an idyllic climate for a good deal of the year and much tourism. In the city centre, Taksim Square leads to the elegant street of Cumhuriyet Caddesi, where the tourist information office is located, along with plenty of hotels and shops, while the Republic Squares gardens are close by.

Antalya Tourist Information and Tourism: top Sights

Old Town Antalya is where tourists will find many of the city's oldest attractions, with numerous mosques adding much Turkish character. The city's beaches offer something quite different and are always very busy during the summer, when holiday makers often choose to head to some of the nearby beaches just outside of the city's environs. Antalya's newly opened Beach Park offers fun for all the family, with its Aqualand featuring countless water slides, and the adjoining Dolphinland is home to a collection of dolphins, sea lions and white whales. For a little more history, be sure to check out the ancient cities of Phaselis and Perge (Perga).

During the Middle Ages, the city of Antalya was an important Byzantine stronghold and today, a number of its medieval landmarks remain in a good state of repair. Hadrian's Gate is amongst the most famous and its three beautifully preserved arches once formed the main gateway through the ancient city walls, almost 1,900 years ago. Other important sights within Antalya include both its Fluted Minaret (Yivli Minare) and its Truncated Minaret (Kesik Minare).

Although it is true to say that Antalya is far from overflowing with museums, artefacts and historical information, there are a few such attractions worthy of a little time.

The Antalya Museum (Antalya Müzesi) really does stand out and offers an insight into the city's Roman and Ottoman past. Another good bet is the Suna and Inan Kirac Kaleici Museum, while close by, further museums await in the neighbouring seaside resort city of Alanya.

There is a truly extraordinary selection of tourist attractions situated on the outskirts of Antalya, including spectacular Roman remains, picturesque stretches of coastline and national parks. For the most impressive ruins, a day trip to either Patara or Termessos won't disappoint. Antalya is also within reach of the port town of Bodrum, the Turkish capital of Ankara, and the cosmopolitan city of Istanbul, as well as popular tourist destinations such as Aspendos, Izmir, Kemer, Olimpos (Olympos) and Demre - the home town of the world-famous Saint Nicholas of Myra, who to most is perhaps best known as simply Santa Claus.

Guide to Antalya

Antalya Orientation

The Turkish city of Antalya lies on the south-westerly coastline of Turkey and next to the Mediterranean Sea, where it is home to almost 800,000 people. Located within the Antalya Province where it has become the capital city, Antalya stands high above the seafront, on top of a steep cliff.

Many scenic mountains surround the city and offer a particularly beautiful and natural backdrop on the north, east and west sides, while the Gulf of Antalya lies directly to the south. The city itself is based around a series of coastal plains, with the Kepezüstü Plain standing alongside the city centre and comprising an important residential area.

The main entrance into Antalya is via the 'gate of the city', which is better known locally as the 'Kalekapisi' and lies in the historical Old Quarter of Kaleici. Many tourists will find that the Kaleici district is the most appealing part of the city and its quays and harbour walls have all been recently restored, along with its imposing mosque. The Sarampol part of Kaleici is where you will find a good pedestrianised shopping area.

Trams fully encircle this part of Antalya and also travel along the actual seafront, linking the main places of interest and Turkish attractions. Head to the south and you will come upon the harbour, or to the west to reach the waterfront street of Cumhuriyet Caddesi, which leads to the Akdeniz Bulvari and ultimately the Konyaalti Beach. For maps of Antalya, look out for the tourist office on the Cumhuriyet Caddesi. Here you will find free city maps, although only a fairly

limited offering of available accommodation leads.

Alanya - south-east.   Ankara - north-east.

Bodrum west.   Burdur north.

Cirali - south-west.   Denizli - north-west.

Fethiye west.   Isparta north.

Istanbul north.   Izmir - north-west.

Karaman east.   Kemer - south-west.

Konya - north-east.   Korkuteli - north-west.

Kumluca - south-west.   Manavgat east.

Mersin - south-east.   Olimpos (Olympos) south.

Patara - south-west.   Serik east.

Seydisehir - north-east. Side east.

Termessos - north-wes.

Antalya Weather and Climate

The climate of Antalya remains fairly mild throughout the year, meaning that the city enjoys a steady flow of visitors outside of the hot summer months. Antalya is certainly best known for its sunny weather and high summer temperatures, which regularly rise above 30°C / 86°F between June and September, and at times reach 35°C / 95°F.

However, the high levels of humidity can make the summer climate feel even hotter, together with the noticeable lack of northerly winds. Therefore many Antalya sightseers favour an early start to the day, cooling down in the sea or water parks later on.

Seasonal Climate Variations / When To Go

During the fine summer weather, the waters around Antalya quickly warm up and tend to stay around 28°C / 82°F, and so are very inviting to swimmers, while those who prefer to worship the Turkish sun can simply lie back on the beach.

The climate begins to cool down slowly, from October onwards, and as the winter months approach, the likelihood of rainy weather increases. However, once the rainy weather season arrives in Antalya, anytime from November to March, it generally only lasts a matter of weeks and is interspersed with fine days and blue skies. December, January and February are always the coldest months in Antalya, although with daytime temperatures averaging 15°C / 59°F or 16°C / 61°F, and nights usually remaining well above freezing, snow is virtually unheard of.

Antalya Weather And Climate Chart (Averages)

Antalya Turkey Travel Guide

	Maximum	Minimum
January	15°C / 59°F	5°C / 41°F
February	16°C / 61°F	6°C / 43°F
March	17°C / 63°F	7°C / 45°F
April	21°C / 70°F	11°C / 52°F
May	26°C / 79°F	16°C / 61°F
June	30°C / 86°F	20°C / 68°F
July	33°C / 91°F	23°C / 73°F
August	32°C / 90°F	22°C / 72°F
September	30°C / 86°F	19°C / 66°F
October	26°C / 79°F	16°C / 61°F
November	20°C / 68°F	11°C / 52°F
December	16°C / 61°F	6°C / 43°F

Antalya Airport Guide

Located a mere 10 km / 6 miles east from the Antalya city centre, Antalya International Airport (AYT) is situated on Turkey's Mediterranean Coast. Close to Yesilkoy, Buyukkumluca, Calkaya and Guzeloba, this facility operates an international, domestic and cargo terminal.

AYT Airport serves approximately 25 million passengers annually, most of whom are incoming tourists, arriving for sun, sea, sand and general Antalya holidays. Turkey's primary airport and the Mediterranean's number two after Mallorca, Antalya regularly appears within the top 100 list of worldwide airports and has experienced tremendous growth over the past decade. Amidst much publicity, the tender for passenger terminals has recently been awarded to Fraport and also the IC Group.

The airport is connected to Antalya city centre via the D400 road (Gazi Bulvan) and the journey takes approximately 20 minutes by car. Taxis can be hired from a rank outside of the Arrivals Hall, and the Havas Airport Shuttle Bus offers service to several of the city's major hotels as well as to the city centre. From the city of Antalya, transport along the surrounding coastline and into the countryside can be arranged, with the main destinations including Alanya, Korkuteli, Kumluca, Manavgat and Serik.

About Antalya Tourism

Antalya has been called 'the capital of Turkey's tourism', and it sits on a cliff in the midst of mountains and forests, set against the backdrop of the Mediterranean Sea. Located on the south-western side of Turkey and next to the Mediterranean Sea, the city of Antalya boasts ancient ruins, a nearby yacht harbour, and an archaeological museum.

Antalya Airport (AYT) is a gateway to the many coastal resorts of Turkey, such as Alanya, Anamur and Manavgat, which boasts more than 60 km / 37 miles of coastline and many beautiful sandy beaches. Seafood restaurants are plentiful around the main seaside resorts, using freshly caught fish from the nearby waters of the Mediterranean.

Antalya Airport is a busy air facility that serves one of Turkey's most popular holiday destinations. It now ranks amongst the largest and busiest hubs in the south-western pocket of Turkey. More than 25 million passengers are catered for at this airport each year, most of whom come for the surf, sun and fun of Antalya.

There are two terminals serving international passengers, as well as one domestic terminal. Three runways are in operation, with two measuring some 3,400 metres / 11,150 feet in length. The first international terminal was built in 1996, while the second was added recently. Some of the destinations served by airlines using the airport include Cologne, Helsinki, Paris, Sofia and Rome.

Freebird Airlines, Pegasus Airlines, Sky Airlines and Turkish Airlines all use Antalya Airport as their principal hub. The complex receives seasonal, charter and scheduled flights year-round. It stands to the east of the city's downtown district and close to the suburbs of Guzeloba, Calkaya and Kemeragzi, with buses and taxis transporting passengers to nearby locations.

Antalya Airport (Ayt)
Address: Highway D400, Antalya, Turkey

Tel: +90 242 330 3600

Passengers can easily reach downtown Antalya, which is located 10 km / 6 miles from the airport. Drivers can take the D400 as far as the Aspendos Boulevard, which connects with downtown Antalya, one of the country's premier holiday spots.

Facilities:

- ✓ Numerous currency exchanges
- ✓ Elevators and escalators
- ✓ Over a dozen baby care rooms
- ✓ Banks and ATMs in both terminals, providing a 24-hour service
- ✓ Food outlets and restaurants, such as Via Café, Popeyes and Sera Café

- ✓ Duty free shopping operated by Nuance-Net
- ✓ Car hire with reliable companies such as Filo Rent, Hertz, Budget and Avis
- ✓ Tourist welcome and information desks
- ✓ Elevators and escalators for passengers with limited mobility
- ✓ Short-term (multi-storey) parking and long-term parking (minimum of four days) with courtesy transfer service

Cars And Taxis
The airport is located close to the centre of Antalya, meaning that catching a taxi or driving oneself into the city are both equally good options. Take the D400 from the airport to the eastern periphery of the city. Turn onto the Aspendos Boulevard to reach the heart of Antalya. Of note, taxis are available 24 hours and operate from all terminals.

Buses

Buses are cheaper than taxis and run between 06:10 and 01:10 every day. These regular buses generally take about 20 minutes to reach downtown Antalya, while select airlines provide buses for passengers. Havas, a popular coach service to the city, runs via the D400 and leaves from the Domestic Terminal.

Airport Hotels and Accommodation

Antalya is one of the most beautiful spots in Turkey and is located in the Antalya Province. Enjoying a coastal setting alongside the Mediterranean Sea, this is a sprawling city and contains many popular hotels, with accommodation located both along the shoreline and close to Antalya International Airport (AYT).

There are no hotels available on the airport grounds, but transport to nearby hotels is easily arranged through hotel shuttle buses. Amongst the nearest hotels to Antalya Airport, the Best Western Khan Hotel contains 120 guest rooms and located within the heart of the city, near to a large shopping centre

The Divan Talya Hotel Antalya and the Sheraton Voyager Antalya Hotel are both roughly 12 km / 7 miles from the airport and situated seaside on the Mediterranean. Further accommodation can be found in the city centre, together with a number of additional Mediterranean resorts located in close proximity to the city.

During the summer months, accommodation is at a premium, with more than one million tourists visiting the Antalya region. Many popular hotels are based around the main marina area and often boast elevated views.

Within the centre of Antalya you will find a range of accommodation, including guest houses and hotels, both old and new. The central Kaleici area is particularly charming, with a rustic character, cobblestone streets and a number of historic Turkey buildings, together with many shops and restaurants aimed at the buoyant tourist market.

History Overview

A modern airport and a relatively new addition to the aeronautical scene in Turkey, Antalya International Airport had struggled to meet demands until in the mid-1990s, a new international terminal was planned. The airport was transformed when it opened its terminal doors at the beginning of April 1998 and began attracting many significant airlines, serving around two million passengers that year.

By the year 2000, more than nine million people were flying in and out of Antalya Airport, which meant that the airport was listed amongst the 100 largest in the whole world. A second runway has recently been constructed and it is expected that future passenger numbers will soon top 25 million per annum. Antalya International Airport (AYT) is currently managed by the Fraport and IC Holding group.

Facilities at Antalya Airport are widespread and there are a wide range of shopping and duty-free options, in both the arrivals and departures areas. Popular shops sell designer clothes and sunglasses, jewellery, scarves and more. Particularly popular is Turkish Delight, a confectionary shop selling a range of traditional Turkish sweets, and there is even a Turkish Bazaar, perfect for that last-minute gift.

Antalya Airport is also home to several ATMs, a bureau de change, public telephones, information desks and a wide range of restaurants, cafés and bars, which are spread around check-in, the gate area and arrivals. There is everything here from American-style fast food to sandwiches, cappuccino and even cold beer, at the Carizou's Cafe and the Park Cafe.

Airlines, Terminals and Facilities

Antalya International Airport is divided into two passenger terminals and one cargo terminal. The international terminal handles approximately 40 per cent of Turkey's air traffic, and carriers such as Cyrus Airlines serve passengers to several destinations across Europe and beyond.

The Arrivals Hall and the Departures Hall both house an information desk. Duty-free outlets provide a wide range of products, as do several gift shops, newsagents and tobacconists.

The Oasis Café is located near the check-in area and sells soft drinks, alcoholic beverages and snacks. Other dining options include a Burger King, the Cola Can, and a German Pub.

A bureau de change located in the International Arrivals zone offers poor exchange rates, and travellers holding foreign currency may be better served by exchanging their money at their hotel. Several ATMs are situated throughout both passenger terminals. Limited business facilities are available in the CIP lounge.

More comprehensive business and conference facilities can be found at the nearby Divan Talya

Hotel Antalya and the Sheraton Voyager Antalya Hotel. Other airport facilities include a prayer room, baby-changing facilities and card-operated telephones.

Antalya International Airport caters for disabled passengers. Wheelchairs are available at the information desk, lifts are spacious and accessible to wheelchairs, and restrooms are equipped with adapted toilets. Worth noting, airport personnel offer boarding assistance upon request.

Terminal 1

Adria Airways.	Aeroflot.	Aeroflot (Donavia).	Aeroflot (Rossiya).
Aerosvit Airlines.	Air Astana.	Air Bashkortostan.	Air Berlin.
Air Bucharest.	Air Mediterranee.	Air Moldova.	Air Onix.

Antalya Turkey Travel Guide

airBaltic.	Arkefly.	Armavia.	Atlasjet.
Aurela.	Austrian Airlines (Lauda Air).	Azerbaijan Airlines.	Belair.
Belle Air.	Bingo Airways.	Bulgaria Air.	Bulgarian Air Charter.
Condor.	Corendon Airlines.	Corendon Dutch Airlines.	Dniproavia.
Donbassaero.	EasyJet.	Edelweiss Air.	Enter Air.
Europe Airpost.	Finnair.	FlyGeorgia.	Freebird Airlines.
Georgian Airways.	Germania.	Germanwings.	Hamburg Airways.
Holidays Czech Airlines.	I-Fly.	Iraqi Airways.	Jat Airways.
Jetairfly.	Jettime.	Kolavia.	Livingston.
Lufthansa.	Luxair.	Monarch Airlines.	Moskovia Airlines.
Neos.	Niki.	Nordwind Airlines.	Norwegian Air Shuttle.
Novair.	Onur Air.	Orenair.	Pegasus

			Airlines.
Polet Airlines.	Primera Air.	Red Wings Airlines.	RusLine.
S7 Airlines.	S7 Airlines (Globus).	SAMair.	Scandinavian Airlines.
SCAT.	Sky Airlines.	Small Planet Airlines.	SmartLynx Airlines.
SmartWings.	SunExpress.	SunExpress (SunExpress Deutschland).	Swiss International Air Lines (Edelweiss Air).
Tailwind Airlines.	TAROM.	Tatarstan Airlines.	Thomas Cook Airlines.
Thomas Cook Airlines Belgium.	Thomas Cook Scandinavia.	Thomson Airways.	Transaero Airlines.
Transavia.com.	Transavia.com France.	Travel Service Airlines.	TUIfly.
TUIfly Nordic.	Turkish Airlines.	Ukraine International Airlines.	Ural Airlines.
UTair Aviation.	UTair Ukraine.	VIM Airlines	Wind Rose

Aviation.

Wizz Air Ukraine.

TERMINAL 3

Atlasjet.	Borajet.
Onur Air.	Pegasus Airlines.
Sky Airlines.	SunExpress.
Turkish Airlines.	Turkish Airlines (AnadoluJet).

Airport Transportation

Driving Directions and Car Hire / Rental

The city of Antalya is located on the western side of the airport and is accessible via the D400 Antalya Road, being just a short drive away.

Passengers flying into Antalya International Airport (AYT) can make a quick transit to and from the passenger terminals in only 20 minutes. From Antalya, travel by bus or car can be arranged to other Turkish destinations.

Speed limits in Antalya, Turkey

Urban areas: 50 kph / 30 mph

Open roads: 90 kph / 55 mph

Motorways / highways: 120 kph / 75 mph

Antalya International Airport (Ayt) Airport Car Rental / Car Hire
Antalya Airport houses several car hire firms, situated in the International Arrivals Hall. Cars can be rented on-the-spot upon arrival, but advance booking is recommended. Rental cars are a great way to travel around this part of Turkey, with scenic roads overlooking the coastline and the Antalya Gulf. Close to the airport you will find Aspendos, Manavgat, Perge

and Serik to the west, while Bubon, Genoanda, Kadyna, Saklikent and Tlos are all located to the west.

Antalya Airport is served by the following car hire companies:

- ✓ Sixt
- ✓ Budget
- ✓ Hertz
- ✓ FLO
- ✓ Decar
- ✓ Intercity
- ✓ Europcar
- ✓ Bumerang

Ground Transport and Parking

The Havas airport shuttle bus regularly leaves the airport after all incoming domestic and international flights. Scheduled stops begin with the Falez and Sheraton Voyager hotels, and continue on to a designated stop where passengers may board minibuses to Kemer. The Havas shuttle continues to the Antalya Otogar bus terminal before making its final stop at the city centre.

Taxis hold a monopoly on local transport and may be hired from the rank outside the terminal building, where a signboard displays fixed (and expensive) fares to all local destinations. Fares are calculated in US currency. There is no train service to Antalya Airport. In some cases, hotels and local tour agents may provide transport to a limited list of local destinations.

General Parking Facilities

Two secure parking lots are located in front the two terminal buildings, set amidst a botanical garden. One lot is designated for cars, while the other is set aside for buses and coaches. Roughly 750 long-term spots are conveniently located within walking distance of the terminals.

Disabled passengers will find the parking lots accessible and convenient. Assistance from individual airline staff is available upon request.

Airport Climate and Weather

Antalya features a Mediterranean climate and is situated on the southern coast of Turkey, with much of the area's weather being influenced by the neighbouring Mediterranean Sea. The city of Antalya offers enticing temperatures for much of the year, with hot summers, warm winters and more than 300 days of sunshine annually.

The summer climate in Antalya is at its hottest from June to September, when temperatures average 31°C / 88°F and often top 35°C / 95°F.

Summers generally experience Antalya's driest weather, with low levels of precipitation.

Winters in Antalya tend to be the wettest time of the year, although mild southerly winds keep the daytime temperatures well above 10°C / 50°F, with night-times averaging 6°C / 43°F at this time of the year. The average annual daytime temperatures in Antalya are around 24°C / 74°F.

Climate Description: Mediterranean climate

Antalya Airport (AYT) Location: Northern Hemisphere, Turkey

Annual High / Low Daytime Temperatures at Antalya: 33°C / 15°C (91°F / 59°F)

Average Daily January Temperature: 15°C / 59°F

Average Daily June Temperature: 30°C / 86°F

Annual Rainfall / Precipication Antalya at Airport (AYT): 1055 mm / 42 inches

City Information

Visiting Antalya - What to See and Do
The largest city on the Mediterranean coast of Turkey is Antalya. It serves as the hub for travellers heading to the resorts of the Turkish Riviera, but is also a worthy destination in its own right. The Old Town and its harbour have been around since 150 BC, being a strategic base for maritime commerce and military strongholds for the reigning Mediterranean powers of the day.

In the 1970s, Antalya shifted gears and became the hottest place in Turkey for seaside holidaymaking. Today there are literally thousands of resorts, hotels and pensions (traditional guesthouses) in and around the city, catering to the hoards of travellers who come to enjoy some genuinely wonderful beaches, coastal villages and related attractions.

Enter the Old Quarter through Hadrian's Gate to escape the bustle of the modern city and imagine life here some 2,000 years ago. Antalya has a superb archaeological museum and lots of ancient ruins within easy striking distance. This is one destination where you can get the best of everything - sun, sea, sand, ancient sites and modern amenities.

Ten Things You Must Do In Antalya

- ✓ Your first stop here should be the impressive Antalya Museum, a comprehensive repository of Turkey's rich heritage. More than 5,000 fascinating artefacts are on display in 14 well-arranged exhibit halls, from classic mythology in the Gallery of the Gods to the Sarcophagus

Gallery with its intricate tombs. Another notable attraction is the Byzantine collection, containing priceless religious icons and other marvels of the Christian era.

- ✓ The finest ancient monument in Antalya is Hadrian's Gate. It serves as a gateway into the Old Quarter neighbourhood of Kaleici. It was built in classic Roman style to commemorate the visit of Emperor Hadrian in 130 AD, and it is a miracle that this beautiful piece of architecture is even standing today.

- ✓ A great day adventure is to climb to the ancient Mountaintop Citadel of Termessos. Even Alexander the Great could not conquer this impregnable fortress. You can make the steep climb up the steps to wander the beautiful ruins of the city that include the

Greek Theatre overlooking Antalya below. It is a bit of an effort to get up here, but absolutely worth it.

- ✓ See the coastline and the Old Town of Antalya from a special perspective aboard one of the pleasure boats running cruises along the coast. They run for two, four or six hours and sail around little islets. Each trip varies, from party boats to quiet cruises, so ask about the package and boat before joining. You can show up at the harbour right before morning departures or book a seat the evening before - hawkers ensure you know where to find them.

- ✓ For a day of modern fun, head to the entertaining Antalya Beach Complex at Konyaalti, which comprises the attractions of Dolphinarium, Aqualand and Aquapark.

Between these three big popular amusement parks you will have all the fun and company you could ever want. Around ten beach clubs are also onsite, providing beachside amenities and services to take any hassle out of a day on the sea.

- ✓ The ancient port town of Phaselis is one of the most inspiring excursions from Antalya. It is just 14 km / 9 miles away, and offers a fantastic blend of nature and ancient ambience. Three pristine coves are here for swimming, while pine forests cover the rocky headlands. After a swim, wander the ancient streets of this charming city and dream of days long past.

- ✓ An alternative to bustling Konyaalti is Lara Beach, a 45-minute minibus ride in the opposite direction. Here you will find a dozen beach clubs providing all the usual amenities and water sports. The long sandy stretches of beach here are perfect for strolls, and the swimming is warm and calm. Minibuses provide easy transport from Antalya throughout the day.

- ✓ Spend the evening strolling the waterfront promenade of Konyaalti's Beach Park, where sea breezes create the ideal environment for the sunset. Plenty of cafés line the pathway and suit those looking for an al fresco dinner. Alternatively you can just have a few drinks on the grassy lawns of a local tavern backed by soft cushions and beautiful moonlit views over the sea.

- ✓ The highest concentration of historic character is to be found in the Kaleici neighbourhood, where ancient narrow lanes wind past cafés, shady squares and inviting shops. There are dozens of appealing attractions to be found within this large district, and the place takes on a whole new feel on a moonlit night.

✓ Take a day off the beach to visit the ancient ruins of Perge and Aspendos, within comfortable reach of Antalya. Both can be toured in a single trip and together they will give you a good sense of how the ancient residents once lived. Perge is famous for its huge stadium, while Aspendos has an impressive theatre.

Sightseeing in Antalya

What to see. Complete travel guide
Advantageous geographical location of the city has made it the warmest and the most picturesque resort in Turkey. Just like any old

city, Antalya offers not only magnificent beaches, but also a wide choice of excursion routes.

One of the most attractive and frequently visited places in this city is the Archeology Museum, which was opened in 1972. The halls of this museum contain precious finds discovered during excavations in the 18-20th centuries. Previously these priceless exhibitions were stored in Yivli Mosque until the museum offered a dozen of spacious halls for that purpose. Most probably, the most famous architectural building in Antalya is Hidirlik Kulesi. This tower was built during the Roman Empire times. The historians name several theories concerning the building to this tower. Some assume the tower was built for protective purposes, while the others think this is an ancient lighthouse. There is also a giant square shaped stone inside the tower, which makes the historians think the tower could have been used as a burial vault for one of great kings, because this block reminds a tombstone a lot.

Yivli Minaret remains the symbol of Antalya for several centuries already. The height of this Minaret estimates 38 meters. The Minaret was built in the 13th century. It reminds of a magnificent castle diving in rich greenery and flowers. When it comes to talking about the nature, we must mention Karaalioglu Park, which landscapes remind the stories from Arabian fairy tales. Fine aroma from mandarin groves, wonderful sculptures and fountains create an unforgettable romantic atmosphere. This park has quickly become the most beloved place for couples and it remains the best destination for evening walks and solitary rest. Duden waterfall is also among the most famous natural sights of

Antalya. This waterfall should be visited by every traveler as the view of water cascade falling down from high rocks looks so magnifying that many visitors spend here hours.

There are a number of unique archaeological areas located in the vicinity of Antalya; not more than half an hour drive separates the city from an ancient amphitheatre of Aspendos. More than 2 000 years ago, it was on the territory of a large prosperous city, this vast amphitheatre could simultaneously accommodate up to 50000 spectators. Through the efforts of modern archaeologists, the amphitheatre was rebuilt almost in its original form, and today the restored construction is the venue of important cultural events. Its main feature is the amazing acoustics. Even if it's just a small coin dropped on stage, the sound of its fall will be heard in the back rows.

Not everyone knows that Antalya is not only about the beautiful beaches and water parks, but also has a great ski resort Saklikent. It offers all the conditions for a comfortable stay; on the territory of the resort there are trails of various difficulty levels, sports equipment rental, and ski schools. Here you spend a great couple of days; and for the tourists at the resort there are mini-hotels and various boarding houses.

If you're looking to add some diversify to the excursion program, be sure to visit the Karain cave, which is also located in the immediate vicinity of Antalya. This cave is the archaeological site of world's importance; it is the world's largest monument of Paleolithic times. The first archaeological research began here in 1946, since then they are carried out almost non-stop. The cave was inhabited by humans more than 25 000 years, and here the researchers found unique tools of primitive people, as well as ritual objects and ornaments. Karain Cave is quite large, almost all of its halls today are equipped with special viewing platforms.

One of the most attractive places for families is considered to be the Antalya Zoo. It covers an area of over 300 hectares, and today the zoo features more than 80 animal species on its territory. Visitors will be able to see wild boars and wolves, feed the cute ducks and watch the clever monkeys. This zoo is attractive not only by the variety of animals, but also through an elaborate design. On its territory there are many recreation areas equipped with benches and gazebos, as well as playground for kids and a cosy café.

Family trip with kids

Family trip to Antalya with children. Ideas on where to go with your child
Antalya is a fairly old and very popular resort with developed infrastructure. It is not surprising that entertainment can be found here for every taste, including for children. Here is one of the largest and most interesting water parks in Turkey, "Troy Aqua", which will amaze guests with its impressive scale, variety of attractions and beautiful design. The opening of the water park took place in 2006. It occupies an area of about 12,000 square meters. In this water park, in addition to the classy pools and slides, there are wonderful recreation areas with live plants and unusual thematic decorations. For the

youngest visitors, a special recreation area with children's attractions was put in place. On the territory of the water park, there is a dolphinarium whose visit will also give a lot of unforgettable impressions.

With children, you should definitely visit the Antalya Aquarium. Famous Italian architects and designers worked on its plan. The central part of the aquarium's exposition is a sunken ship, the length of which is 20 meters. Another interesting feature of the aquarium is a transparent tunnel, whose length is 131 meters. A walk on it will be unforgettable. Overhead visitors of the attraction are constantly swimming large sharks, stingrays and exotic fish. In the aquarium, there is also an excellent entertainment center in which there are more than 30 thematic areas. A trip to this unique center of the underwater world promises to be very informative.

Antalya Zoo also deserves special attention. In recent years, it has significantly changed. Here appeared new spacious aviaries. Several artificial lakes were created on the territory of the zoo, in which waterfowl live. Among the main inhabitants of the zoo are fast zebras and Australian kangaroos, flamingos and very cute deer, which are sure to please the youngest visitors. The area of the zoo is 330 hectares. On its territory, there are more than 80 species of animals. The zoo literally drowns in the abundance of greenery. Its territory is equipped with many beautiful recreation areas with benches. Here you can easily find a place in the shade of trees and enjoy the singing of birds.

With older children, it is worth going on an exciting excursion. To its guests, Antalya offers dozens of variants. The most popular excursion is to the Yanartash Mountain, which is also known to many travelers under the unofficial name "Burning Mountain". It is located in Kemer. To reach it will not be difficult for the guests of Antalya. This landmark will be interesting to visit with children of school age. They will be impressed by the majestic mountain, from the slopes of which flames burst out. The spectacle is very impressive, and the secret of the natural phenomenon is very simple - a huge accumulation of gas that leaves through the crevices in the earth. Many interesting legends are associated with Mount Yanartash, which will also impress young travelers.

When on a hot day you want to relax in a beautiful shopping and entertainment center, you should go to OZDILEK. It is the largest shopping and entertainment complex in the city. There is a huge selection of shops, including children's. In addition to the shops in the center, there are excellent cafes, bowling alleys and a cinema. The complex OZDILEK is distinguished and spectacularly decorated. This is only a small part of the entertainment available for travelers with children in sunny Antalya.

Unusual weekend

How to spend top weekend in Antalya - ideas on extraordinary attractions and sites

Köprüçay River Rafting
If you are tired of hot weather and your peaceful vacation in Antalya, consider trying rafting in the

clean mountain river of Köprüçay. It is located in a nature reserve famous for its incredibly beautiful landscapes. The temperature of water in the river is always 14 oC even during a hot day. Before the adventure starts, you will get all the necessary gear and listen to precautions and safety measures.

An experienced instructor will teach you how to control the boat. During rafting, the instructor will be with you and will always be ready to help. Such an adventure lasts from half an hour to three hours depending on the route chosen. In the middle of the way, you will make a stop to relax, enjoy freshly caught fish, and admire the nature. After that, you will continue rafting.

It is better not to take a camera with you because you will hardly have time to take pictures and the expensive device can be damaged by water. As this rafting tour is organized by professionals, when you reach the most spectacular areas of the route, a professional photographer will take several pictures. You will get a series of emotional pictures about this extreme adventure. Moreover, you will get pictures with two picturesque waterfalls and an ancient bridge on the background.

Excursion to the Hidirlik Tower
If you want to see spectacular views of Antalya from the height of 14 meters and find out many interesting facts about the city's landmarks, consider making an excursion to the Hidirlik Tower that has a shape of a drum. In the past, it was showing the way to adventurers and was also used as a fortress. Many consider the tower the most mysterious old construction in Antalya.

According to old documents, the tower had a spiked cupola in the past, but it was destroyed later.

If you come to Hidirlik from the eastern side, you will see a rectangular stone block that weights several tons. The purpose of that stone block is still not clearly known. Many scientists are sure that the building was used for religious purposes because its walls are decorated with beautiful frescoes. You will be able to see them during an excursion.

A narrow ladder with round-shaped steps will take you to the top of the tower. You will have to walk slowly and move closer to the wall because there is a risk of falling down. Having reached the top, you will see the restoration performed yet by the Seljuks during the Middle Ages, admire the spectacular view of the bay and listen to interesting stories about the Hidirlik from the guide

Diving in Antalya
If you are a fan of diving, mild climate and excellent visibility of up to 35 meters deep make it possible to explore the underwater world of the region. Moreover, scuba diving is available all year round here. If you have no experience in scuba diving but would like to try it, there are many diving schools that are ready to teach visitors. You can rent all the necessary gear in one of them as well and hire a professional instructor.

The area between Lara and Konyaalti Beaches is the easiest one, especially if you are a beginner. There are rocky cliffs that are very comfortable and allow diving up to 25 meters deep. There is no strong current, and this area has a beautiful underwater life. You can also try diving near Taşlık burnu. In the past, the cargo ship named Gelidoniya, which was built in the 13th century, sank there after crashing into rocks.

If you dive approximately 1 kilometer away from the city's pierce, you can see another sunken ship, Saint Didier. During the Second World War, this ship delivered equipment and ammo and supplies for battles in the desert. However, in order to dive there, you need to get a special permission from the city's authorities. The region not far from a small island named Sichang is also suitable for diving. There is an underwater cave, but yachts and strong current make it not simple to dive there. On the other hand, many may find it even more interesting that way.

Culture: sights to visit

Culture of Antalya. Places to visit - old town, temples, theaters, museums and palaces

Hıdırlık Kulesi Tower remains one of the most striking monuments of the city. The construction of the tower took place in the 2nd century BC. According to one version, the tower was an important fortification facility designed to protect the port area. Some also believe that it could serve as a beacon, but a part of historians think that Hıdırlık Kulesi is nothing but a tomb of the rulers. The mystery of the ancient tower still keeps bothering the minds of historians and travelers who stroll leisurely along its walls, trying to solve this centuries-old mystery. In Antalya is located one of the most famous museums in the country, the exhibition of which is devoted to priceless archaeological finds. The museum is equipped with more than ten halls, each of which contains collections of unique artifacts.

Previously the majority of the exhibits found here were kept in Yivli Minare, which is also an important object of excursions. The height of the beautiful tower estimates 38 meters. It was built in the 13th century and has perfectly preserved till our days. The beautiful minaret consists of eight half-columns, each of which makes the building look even more spectacular. The building is surrounded by a rich park, which serves as a magnificent background to this ancient monument. Guests of the city should also not forget to visit Hadrian gates, which were built in 130 AD in honor of the great emperor. White columns support three graceful arches. Magnificent plaster cornices have become a really skillful decoration of this grand construction. To please the Emperor, the builders have pictured his coat on the gates. Travellers believe that if you make a wish and pass under the three arcs, your wish will certainly come true.

Fans of natural attractions will be interested in visiting Karaalioglu Park, which is located not far away from the coastline. Here you can stroll through picturesque tangerine groves and admire the beauty of graceful fountains and sculptures. In the evening the park is a favorite place of dates of couples. This is a romantic and a beautiful place that is always full of harmony and peace. An excursion to the Duden Waterfalls will be a no less interesting and exciting activity. There are special observation platforms near the waterfalls, so visitors can easily go behind the flowing veil of sparkling water. These are not all peculiarities of this place as you may enjoy making a visit to a Cave of Wishes. According to one legend, this small cave once was a home to monks who had sought there peace and solitude amongst the natural splendor.

Every large Turkish city is associated with Ataturk the great reformer can either have a monument erected to him, or have a museum dedicated to him, or have a building or street named after him. You can spot a monument to the cult Turkish personality in Antalya. It is located on the Republic Square. There are many fascinating mosques in the city. One of them is Tekeli Mehmet Paşa Mosque which is the major mosque of the city. This is an excellent example of construction of the 16th 17th centuries. The mosque has a mind-blowing interior decoration, which is beautifully illuminated through the stained glass windows. Another interesting monument of sacred architecture is called Iskele Mosque. This mosque was built in the 19th century and, although it is small, the special atmosphere that reigns here always makes it a pleasure to come back.

Antalya is an ancient city, and therefore you can spot many ruins here. Some of them are deserving of attention. First of all, the ancient city of Pisidia is worth a special visit as it preserves the prehistoric ruins reminiscent of ancient Rome, which are mingled with the monuments of the times of the Ottoman Empire. Among the buildings you can find the ramparts of the upper cities, administrative and public buildings, as well as residential buildings. In addition, the sight of the ancient ruins in itself gives pleasurable feeling, as if you were transmitted into history. You can enjoy the beautiful views of the sun-drenched Antalya expanses which open up from here.

Another ruin of the ancient city, Perge, is located in the north-east of Antalya. This is a great place to get acquainted with the local culture. The ruins here are very well preserved, such that you can even picture how the people here once lived and what they did. Above all, let us not fail to mention the amphitheater, the stadium and the main streets these facilities are preserved best among others. All tourists when visiting a place like this are advised to stock up on water, have a hat, and also apply cream with an SPF factor, since there is very little shade here. From this point, you can also see interesting expanses.

In the northwest of the city you can find another ruin, the Termessos. Here you can see the necropolis, and an amphitheater situated at the top, at an altitude of 70 meters. You should definitely climb to it in order to get incredible impressions. It is necessary to follow the same advice as when visiting the previous ruins to take with you water, a hat and sunscreen. Another significant place is the Antalya ancient fortress, which can be found in the Old City near the Saat Kulesi Clock Tower. This monumental building immediately catches the eye, and you will certainly not be able to bypass it.

Attractions & nightlife

Cuisine of Antalya for gourmets. Places for dinner - best restaurants

The name of the restaurant Gizli Bahçe can be literally translated as "Secret Garden". It is located on one of the high cliffs, from which visitors can enjoy amazing panoramic views of the coast. The restaurant specializes in cooking dishes from the national cuisine, but its menu also contains delicacies from the international cuisine. In the evening in Gizli Bahçe plays live music and this place is always full of visitors. Blue Parrot restaurant is a great place for family rest. In the morning the restaurant serves delicious English breakfast, afternoon is the time when visitors are welcome to enjoy various choice of salads and first courses, and in the evening don't hesitate to choose amazing delicacies. The restaurant often hosts engaging evening parties. From time to time huge plasma screens of the restaurant broadcast major sporting events, so Blue Parrot is loved not only by gourmets, but also by sports fans. When it comes to Chinese food restaurants, we should certainly mention China Garden, a part of the tables of which is served on a beautiful terrace. Beijing duck is considered the specialty of the restaurant. Fans of more original dishes will like soup with crab meat, as well as hot crackers made of shrimps with spicy chili sauce.

Fans of French cuisine will simply not find a better restaurant than Marina. Duck in orange sauce with walnuts, salmon roll with caviar and shrimps, seafood with signature saffron sauce these are just a few specialties that always keep the visitors of this restaurant fully delighted. When it is a dessert time, make your choice in favor of tender cakes the menu of the restaurant contains more than several dozen types of them. Stella's Bistro restaurant specializes in cooking Mediterranean food. Here you can try classic Italian lasagna, gentle pizza, as well as select from a large choice of sandwiches and salads.

The restaurant's tables are located on a terrace, so while having their meal visitors can enjoy magnificent picturesque surroundings.

Kral Sofrasi restaurant is located not far away from marina. It will please lovers of Turkish cuisine. Among the most popular dishes of the restaurant is a huge casserole with meat and vegetables seasoned with chili sauce. It is simply impossible to ignore the restaurant named Sim, the menu of which will be appreciated by the followers of the vegetarian diet. The reason for this is in the restaurant's signature dish - stewed vegetables with spices. However, fans of meat delicacies will also find here several suitable dishes.

All ice cream fans should not forget to try Dondurma during their stay in Antalya. This popular dessert only looks like a classic ice cream as it is also served in crunchy cons. That said, the dessert tastes absolutely incredible and it is hard to compare it with anything else. Milk and sugar are the main ingredients of Dondurma, and that is why this dessert really resembles traditional ice cream. However, the dessert contains mastic and salep that make Dondurma quite viscous. Sometimes this dessert is so thick that one can eat it with fork and knife. Travelers will find this unusual specialty in many restaurants in Antalya. Numerous food carts also often sell Dondurma.

Travelers who cannot imagine their life without sweets will be pleasantly surprised with their stay in Antalya. Simply take a stroll to the city's markets that offer all kinds of the most popular pastries in the region. In addition to traditional Locum and Baklava that are familiar to many travelers, it is possible to try many other interesting sweet masterpieces.

Tulumba is a popular national pastry that is made of sweet dough. Tulumba can vary in shape and size. Sometimes it is cut into small sticks. Some chefs prefer to make gorgeous cracknels. It is better to eat this dessert when it is fresh because it slowly loses its original taste during the shelf life.

Pişmaniye is another popular dessert in Antalya that is sold in many cafes and food carts. The dessert resembles cotton candy, but it has more ingredients, such as pistachios, sesame seeds, and many other ingredients. Fans of halva should head to the district of Kaleiçi in Antalya as chefs in this part of the city cook this dessert in accordance with ancient recipes.

Fans of pastries will enjoy traditional buns with sesame that are very popular in Antalya. Travelers will find vendors selling these buns virtually everywhere. Popular buns are delicious and inexpensive. In order to get acquainted with the culinary traditions of Antalya, travelers do not necessarily need to attend expensive restaurants. It is possible to try unique food right on the city's streets and markets.

Antalya Other Attractions

Archaeological Museum in Antalya
Archaeological Museum in Antalya is one of the best venues of its kind in Turkey. The exhibits shown here come from the archaeological sites from Antalya Province and make a great addition after visiting these places. The most important sites represented in this museum are: Karain

cave, ancient city of Perge and the cities of Lykian civilization.

Both the wealth of museum collections and their presentation in spacious, modern interiors encourage the visitors to can spend many hours in this place. The uniqueness of this institution has also been recognized internationally - in 1988 the Council of Europe awarded it with the Museum of the Year Award.

History of the museum

The first museum in Antalya was founded in 1919, just after the First World War. The teacher Süleyman Fikri Erten, who saved many archaeological pieces from looting, decided to create for them an appropriate venue. Initially, the collections were exhibited at the Yivli Minaret mosque, located in the historic Kaleiçi district. In 1972, a new building was constructed, on the western side of the city, and the mosque was transformed into the Ethnographic Museum.

Display halls and collections

The building of the Archaeological Museum in Antalya boasts an exhibition space of 30,000 square meters. The exhibits are arranged in several spacious halls, and some of them are placed in the museum garden. The objects that are in the possession of the museum illustrate many thousands of years of human activity in the region of Antalya. Because of the huge number of exhibits and the vastness of its facilities at least half the day is necessary to fully appreciate its wealth.

Natural History Hall

This small section of the museum displays the fossils and animal bones from different geological epochs. The most interesting specimens are: the shells of huge snails, the fossils of extinct cephalopods, foraminifera shells and anthozoans.

Pre-History Hall

This hall exhibits the finds from Paleolithic, Mesolithic, Chalcolithic, Neolithic and early Bronze Age. The displayed items are mostly bone and stone tools. Illustrative panels explain the production process of these tools. There is also an exhibition demonstrating the process of leather tanning.

The main focus of this exhibition is on the objects from Karain cave, but there are also some finds from Öküzini and Sehahöyük. One of the most beautiful exhibits is a figure of a woman, found in Hacılar Höyük, Burdur Province.

An extremely interesting feature of this exhibition is the reconstructed urn burial from Karataş-Semayük site near the town of Elmalı. On this site an early Bronze Age cemetery was found where people were buried in clay vessels placed underground.

Halls of Ceramics and Small Objects

These spacious rooms are dedicated to the presentation of small finds dating back to the period from 14th century BC to 15th century AD. The exhibits are ordered thematically and chronologically - there are special sections devoted to the Geometric (the 9th-7th centuries BC), Archaic and Classical (the 7th-5th centuries

BC) periods as well as Roman and Byzantine eras (the 5th-15th centuries AD).

The majority of space is taken by the ceramic finds, beautifully presented and well described. The panels explain the application of such vessels as crater, pyxis, kylix and skyphos.

The second section of this exhibition is devoted to particular archaeological sites from Antalya region. They are illustrated by various finds - clay and glass vessels as well as bronze objects and gold jewelery.

Moreover, the profiles of the best-renown researchers that devoted their lives to the studies of this region are presented, including Thomas Marksteiner, Jürgen Borchhardt, Arif Müfid Mansel and Fahri Işık. They conducted their research in nearby archaeological sites of Myra, Limyra, Patara, Perge and Side.

Mosaic Hall

The center of this hall is used to display ancient mosaics that were found in Lycia region, in Seleukeia and Xanthos. The walls are lined with the statues from various locations, including Hermes and Meleager from Perge and a woman from Rhodiapolis. The most stunning exhibit from this section is a three-headed statue of Hekate, the goddess of the underworld, excavated in Pisidian Antioch.

Heads and Portraits Hall

The separate room of the museum is devoted to the exhibition of marble heads well-known and anonymous men and women from the ancient world. These heads were collected in numerous archaeological sites, including Perge, Patara, Letoon and are dated from the 2nd to the 4th century AD.

Emperors and Gods Halls

These two halls usually make the best impression on the visitors. They are exclusively devoted to the presentation of the statues from Perge excavations. Most of these statues date back to the 2nd century AD.

In the center of Emperors Hall there are the statues of Three Graces and a dancing woman. Along the walls of this room splendidly preserved statues of Roman emperors are displayed, together with their wives and other important figures. Emperor Hadrian sternly observes the visitors and is easily recognized by his trimmed beard. Actually, there are three statues of this emperor in the hall - two of them present him in full armor and one is classically naked. The beard of Lucius Verus is even more impressive, but unfortunately not much has been preserved from his statue.

Emperor Trajan is depicted in beautiful armor and, in contrast to Hadrian, clean-shaven. Septimius Severus was portrayed in a playful mood, quite surprising for an emperor known for his serious attitude to life. The imposing statue of a woman is actually dedicated to Plankia Magna who played a significant role in the development of Perge in the golden age of the city.

The Hall of Gods, as its name implies, is dedicated to the statues of ancient gods and goddesses. They were also made in Perge, in the 2nd century AD, but in majority are just the copies of older, Greek statues. Naked Apollo stares dispassionately into the distance, Artemis - the goddess of hunting - has lost her bow, Athena's breasts are covered with a buckler from leather scales, with the head of Medusa in its center.

Beside the gods from the classical, Greco-Roman pantheon, such as Nemesis and Hygieia, there are also Egyptian gods on display. Serapis does not look especially happy, but this impression might be the result of the missing nose. He is accompanied by Isis, however the only trace of her baby Horus are his legs.

Perge Theatre Hall

A separate museum exhibition is devoted to architectural elements and statues that once adorned the theater in Perge. Many of these statues demonstrate admirable dynamics: Heracles is flexing his muscles, Emperor Trajan is standing nonchalantly, the god of wine - Dionysus - is holding his head, probably sore from too much liquor, only Alexander the Great is standing proudly, like the statues from the Archaic period.

The central part of the exhibition is a statue of a satyr Marsyas, and the walls of the exhibition hall are decorated with the reliefs depicting various scenes from mythology.

Sarcophagus Hall

The wealth represented by the sarcophagi in this room can make you feel dizzy. These exhibits represent the three main groups of Anatolian sarcophagi. The first group is called Pamphylian is can be recognized by distinctive garlands and the figures of Nike and Eros. They were made in workshops in Perge, and then exported to all corners of the Roman Empire, including Rome.

The second group is called Sidemara or sarcophagi with columns. It is most common of the sarcophagi found in Asia Minor, and those that are in museum collections come from Pamphylia region. These sarcophagi are characterized by their decorations reminiscent of the temple with a colonnade. Between the columns, in the form of reliefs, the scenes from the life of the deceased are shown. The most interesting specimen of this kind of sarcophagi displayed in the museum, shows the Labours of Hercules. Another wonderful example is the sarcophagus of Domitias Julianus and his wife, made in the 2nd century AD.

The most unique sarcophagus in the collection of the museum is the one with medallions. This is only one of its kind preserved in its entirety, decorated with medallions supported by the carved figurines of the goddess Nike.

Additionally, there are sarcophagi for children and one, extremely rare, prepared especially for a dog. A separate part of the exhibition is devoted to the funeral customs of the ancient period. Some attention is also devoted to the exhibition of monumental tomb of the king of Lycia - Pericles - from Limyra, the 4th century BC.

Icons Hall

The icons collected in this part of the museum exhibition come from the region of Antalya and are dated to the period from the 18th to the 19th century. The collected icons are a valuable witness to the presence of the Greeks in the region of Antalya, which ended with the population exchange between Turkey and Greece in the 20s of the 20th century. These icons depict the scenes from the activity of Jesus, the Last Judgement, the Ascension of Mary and the life of John the Baptist.

Hall of Coins

The coins displayed in the museum include the pieces from antiquity, the Middle Ages and the modern era. Particular attention of the visitors should be paid to the coin collections or treasures that had been buried for centuries and later discovered intact by archaeologists. A great example of this category is the treasure of Aspendos, which consists of 206 silver staters (Greek coins). These staters, found by archaeologists, were minted in Aspendos, and the latest of them is dated to 350 BC. It is believed that the owner hid his treasure after hearing the news of Alexander the Great approaching the city in 332 BC.

Ethnographic and Turkish - Islamic Period Works Halls

The section devoted to ethnographic topics represents a small part of museum collections and seems to have been prepared without the spirit. There are carpets, traditional costumes, weapons, tiles from the Seljuk and Ottoman periods, manuscripts, candlesticks, a large collection of wooden spoons, and even a horse-drawn vehicle. The most interesting elements of this exhibition are the recreated the interior of a typical household of Antalya from the 19th century and the nomadic tent.

Children's section

In a hall specially prepared for the youngest visitors there are miniature models of the most important historical monuments in Turkey. Children can see the ruins of ancient cities of Perge, Aspendos and Patara, take a look into Karain Cave or a household from Çatalhöyük as well as the fortifications of Alacahöyük or admire the Lycian rock tombs of Myra.

Museum Garden

In the garden of the museum there are mainly stone artifacts from the Roman period, which due to their large size could not be accommodated inside the building.

Getting there:

Archaeological Museum in Antalya is located in the south-western part of the city at Konyaaltı

Caddesi No:1. The distance to the museum from the historical center of Antalya (i.e. Kaleiçi district) is 2.5 km (1.5 mile).

Next to the museum there is the terminal station of a so-called Nostalji Tramvay (Nostalgic Tramway) line that connects the western districts of Antalya with its historical center and the eastern beach district of Lara. The trams run every half an hour, from 7:00 a.m.to 9:00 pm. The regular ticket costs 1.70 TL.

Visitor tips:

Archaeological Museum in Antalya is open every day, in summer season (from April to October) from 9:00 a.m. to 6:30 p.m. In winter season (from November to March) the visiting hours are: 8:00 a.m. to 5:00 p.m. The ticket costs 20 TL (in 2015).

There is a possibility of renting an audio-guide (10 TL) that offers an opportunity to listen to the detailed narratives concerning all museum exhibitions. This system is available in English, Turkish, French, German, Italian, Russian and Spanish. This solution is highly advisable as some of the exhibits have information panels in Turkish only.

Atatürk's House Museum in Antalya

Atatürk's House (tr. Atatürk Evi ve Müzesi) is a museum that aims at commemoration of the visits to Antalya of the first president of the Turkish Republic in the 30s of the 20th century. Although the current building is just a replica of the house where Atatürk actually stayed, the exhibitions inside may prove to be very enlightening, especially concerning the attitude of the Turks to Atatürk and his vision.

Atatürk in Antalya

Mustafa Kemal Atatürk arrived to Antalya for the first time in March of 1930 with a very vital reason - he was just staying in Izmir, but the weather was extremely cold, so he decided to flee to the south for warmth and sunshine. Sounds familiar, doesn't it?

The itinerary of the president ran through Isparta and Burdur, and he reached Antalya on the 6th of March, entering it from the side of Kepez, then a separate town, and now - a district of Antalya. If you ever go along this route, while returning to the Mediterranean coast from a trip to Pamukkale, be sure to find in a spot where the road turns left. You will be rewarded with quite an unusual view, commemorating the journey of Atatürk. The rock wall next to the road was carved in the shape of his face, next to which water cascades from a cliff, and on the other side of the monument the most famous words that Atatürk said about Antalya are written: "Without a doubt, Antalya is the most beautiful place in the world!" (tr. *Hiç Şüphesiz ki Antalya Dünyanın En Güzel Yeridir!*).

In Antalya Atatürk was enthusiastically welcomed by its inhabitants. Along the route, from Kepez to the center, people lined up to see the great leader with their own eyes. The joy was so great that, as a commemorative gift Atatürk received a whole villa just for himself. From its balcony he gave a speech and expressed his gratitude. However, he did not stay in this house for too long, because on the 12th of March he decided to return to Ankara.

During his stay in Antalya Atatürk spent the time visiting museums and ruins of ancient cities and, surprisingly, farmlands - hardly anyone knows that farming and agriculture became his hobby later in life. As a part of an intensive program he also came to Aspendos, where he was deeply moved by the deplorable state of the Roman theater. President's rebuke about this state of affairs quickly brought positive results, as the theater was restored and adapted to the organization of concerts and other cultural events.

Except for a brief visit to Antalya during a sea voyage by steamboat to Silifke, Atatürk's came to the city for the second time in February of 1935. This time the president sailed into the harbor and stopped for the night at his villa and in the evening the next day he sailed to Taşucu. In total he spent at his house in this city just seven nights.

Atatürk's House Museum

After Atatürk's death in 1938 his villa in Antalya was transformed into the Institute for Girls. In 1984 the building was given to the Turkish Ministry of Culture and Tourism, in order to transform it into a museum. Unfortunately, this decision coincided with the planned reconstruction of roads in the city and the building was demolished to make way for an widened Işıklar street. The villa was later rebuilt farther from the road and in 1986 opened to the public as a museum.

The villa is a two-storey house, with a living room, a bathroom, a kitchen and several other rooms located on the ground floor. There are seven rooms, including one with a balcony, on the second floor. Today, on the ground floor there is and exhibition of newspaper clippings and photographs devoted to Atatürk's visits in Antalya.

On the first floor the presidential bedroom and two offices are recreated. In addition, there is a large collection of postage stamps, coins and stamps bearing the likeness of the president. The core of the exhibition consists of personal items (including clothing and shoes), which belonged to Atatürk. They were transported to Antalya from Anıtkabir - the mausoleum of Atatürk in Ankara.

Getting there:

Atatürk's House Museum is situated on Işıklar Caddesi, in the center of Antalya. It can be reached by tram - Nostalji Tramvay line runs right next to the museum, and the nearest stop is called Belediye.

On foot you can visit the museum while strolling through Karaalioğlu park or visiting Kaleiçi district. The distance from Hadrian's Gate to Atatürk's House Museum is only 500 meters.

Visitor tips:

The museum is open to visitors daily except Mondays. From April to October, it is open from 9:00 am to 7:30 pm and in the winter - from 8:30 am to 5:30 pm. The admission to the museum is free of charge.

Broken Minaret in Antalya

The building now known as the Broken Minaret (tr. *Kesik Minare*) hides more secrets that one might have expected. This characteristic structure of an actually broken minaret belongs to the ruined Korkut Mosque (tr. *Korkut Camii*). The history of this building is an excellent illustration that offers a better understanding of the turbulent history of Antalya.

Historical overview

The building, which is currently called the Broken Minaret, was built in the 2nd century AD, in the period of Roman rule, as the temple in classic architectural style. In the Byzantine era, in the 7th century AD, the temple was demolished and rebuilt as a church dedicated to the Virgin Mary (gr. *Παναγία*). During its construction many architectural elements of the ancient temple, including stone blocks and column capitals, were used. During the Arab invasions in the 7th century the church was badly damaged, and had to wait for its renovation until the 9th century.

When, at the beginning of the 13th century, the southern coast of Asia Minor was conquered by the Seljuk Turks, who had their capital in Konya, the Virgin Mary church was quickly converted into a mosque. During this time a minaret was added to the temple. Later, in 1361, Peter I - the king of Cyprus and titular king of Jerusalem, took Antalya over from the Seljuks, the building became a church once again.

This did not stop the trials and tribulations of the temple. The rule of Cyprus in Antalya ended just after twelve years and the Seljuks returned to the city. In 1423 Antalya became a part of the Ottoman Empire. Only then, in the early 16th century, when Antalya was governed by prince Şehzade Korkut, the son of Sultan Bayezid II, the building once again assumed the role of the mosque. From that moment on it was known as Korkut mosque. In 1896 the mosque was destroyed by fire and has never been rebuilt. In

1975 some provisional works were carried out on its premises, but so far no decision has been made about its renovation.

Visitor tips:

The area of Broken Minaret is currently fenced off, but its most important fragments are clearly visible. The building remains the most characteristic orientation point in this area of Kaleiçi district.

Getting there:

Kaleiçi district, where Broken Minaret is located, is a traffic restricted zone, therefore the building is best reached on foot. Broken Minaret is situated on Hesapçı Sokak street, which crosses the district, starting from Hadrian's Gate and finishing near Hıdırlık Tower. The ruined temple is about 400 meters away from Hadrian's Gate and only 200 meters away from Hıdırlık Tower.

City Walls of Antalya

Until the 50s of the 20th century, the word Antalya was understood as only one part of today's city, that being its oldest district, known as Kaleiçi. Karol Lanckoroński, who visited Antalya in the late 19th century, described this area in the following words: "The city outlines a horseshoe shape around the angle of the bay and lies on the ground significantly higher up from the coast platform. Its part is closed tightly by the ramparts, with narrow streets and single districts divided by other walls. [...] The only thing that remained on its original place, as far as we know, are the city walls around the city, although often rebuilt and restored over the centuries". Next Lanckoroński presents a plan of

Antalya, where two lines of city walls are visible: one in the form of a semicircle around the port, and the second, much larger, around whole Kaleiçi district.

Historical overview

Defensive walls of Antalya were built in the Hellenistic period, and the history of their renovation and expansion illustrates the history of the city itself, passing under the dominion of successive empires controlling Asia Minor. In Roman times the walls were first renovated and decorated with numerous towers and gates, of which the greatest was the Hadrian's Gate, well preserved to our times.

In the 8th and the 9th century Antalya became a battleground between Arab and Byzantine armies. Finally, the rulers of Constantinople won and quickly repaired and strengthened the city fortifications. Further renovation took place in the mid-12th century, after the Second Crusade, during the reign of the Byzantine Emperor Manuel I Comnenus.

In 1207 Antalya was taken over by the Seljuk Turks, who immediately began to strengthen the fortifications. In the 13th century four towers were built, three of them are partly preserved, and the fourth one was destroyed in the early 20th century. From this destroyed tower a huge inscription remained, now in the collections of the Archaeological Museum in Antalya.

When, in 1361, the king of Cyprus, Peter I, conquered Antalya after a quick attack from the sea, the walls were decorated by the carvings of coats of arms, similar to those found in the

Castle of St. Peter in Bodrum. Currently, these decorations are also in the local museum.

Antalya finally came under Ottoman control in 1387, and the walls were rebuilt again and again at the behest of successive sultans, including - Mahmud II, in the early 19th century. Even 70 years ago almost all the walls were well preserved, despite the battles fought over the city, numerous insurgencies and earthquakes.

The most accurate description of the ramparts of Antalya was given by Karol Lanckoroński. He mentions 54 towers and perfectly preserved sections of the walls surrounding the old town. Unfortunately, his efforts directed toward the examination of the fortifications were severely hampered both by the dense architecture of the town, as well as the suspicion of the Turkish authorities, reluctant to give permission to foreigner attempting to measure the walls.

Since the late 19th century until the 80s of the 20th century the process of destruction of the walls continued. On the one no maintenance was carried out during this period, and on the other - long stretches of the walls that impeded the development of the city were intentionally demolished. A curious explanation given by the municipal government about the damage done to the ancient fortifications, stated that the people from Kaleiçi district needed more access to fresh air. In fact, the stones collected from the walls were used to build mansions outside the historic quarter and the fate of the walls was completely ignored. As a result only seven towers and several sections of the walls have been preserved to our times.

Getting there:

In order to see the preserved sections of Antalya city walls, visit Kaleiçi district. Near the beautifully restored Hadrian's Gate there is a long section of walls along Atatürk Boulevard. You can get there on foot, walking through Kaleiçi district, or by tram. Nostalji Tramvay line runs along this stretch of the walls, and the most convenient stop is called Hadrian.

Another well-preserved part of the ramparts is Hıdırlık Tower, standing at the seaside, at the point where the historic Kaleiçi district is adjacent to a large Karaalioğlu park. It is located at the end of Hesapçı Sokak street, which crosses the Kaleiçi district, and starts from the Hadrian's Gate. Hıdırlık Tower is 600 just meters away.

Hadrian's Gate in Antalya

Antalya's most beautiful monument is undoubtedly the monumental gate leading into the Kaleiçi. It is called the Hadrian's Gate (tr. *Hadriyanüs Kapisi*) or the Triple Gate (tr. *Üçkapılar*). The first name is a memorial of the ancient history of the city, when, in the second century AD, it was visited by the Roman Emperor Hadrian, while the second term refers to the appearance of the monument, which has three archways.

History of the structure

Hadrian's Gate was built in 130 AD to commemorate the visit of Emperor Hadrian in Attaleia, as Antalya was known in this period. It was incorporated in the walls surrounding the city, and has become a major gateway to the city.

Fantastic stories are told about the gate, like the one about Makeda, Queen of Sheba, who drove through the gate, and then rested in Aspendos, on her way to a meeting with King Solomon. However, there is not a grain of truth in it since these events, even if they had been real, happened in the tenth century BC, and therefore long before the construction of the gate.

Two towers, standing on both sides of the gate, come from different periods of history. Southern tower (the one on the left looking from the Atatürk Boulevard) is from the Roman era, but it was, most probably, built independently from the gate. The architectural distinctness of the tower seems to confirm this theory. This structure is called the tower of Julia Sancta, and its ancient origins are testified by a stone inscription.

The northern tower (on the right) was rebuilt during the reign of the Seljuk sultan Alaeddin Keykubat I, that is, in the first half of the thirteenth century AD. Only its lowest part has been preserved from Roman times. There is also an inscription on this tower, written in Old Turkish language, but in Arabic script.

Hadrian's Gate was discovered for the Western world by Francis Beaufort who, in 1817, published its description in his diary of the trip along the southern coast of Asia Minor. This text contains information about a higher level of the gate. However, it must have been destroyed later in the 19th century, as other European visitors to Antalya, Charles Texier (in the 30s of the 19th century) and Lanckoronski, were no longer able to describe its exact appearance.

At the end of the 19th century, the state of Hadrian's Gate preservation was described the Polish explorer Karol Lanckoronski in these words: *Today it is buried to a depth of several feet, and only visible from the outside, because its internal façade is surrounded by new buildings. The monument is relatively well preserved thanks to the special circumstances i.e. that it has long been obscured by a wall that covered the façade of the exterior and the gap was barely made a couple of years ago*. To the same researcher we also owe a precise description of the entire visible structure and its accurate drawings and plans, made by his companion, George Niemann.

Although it may be hard to believe, the total exposure of Hadrian's Gate and its renovation took place only in the 50s of the twentieth century, over 60 years after the visit of Lanckoronski. Currently, it is one of the highlights of a visit to Antalya and the place where almost every tourist wants to take a commemorative photo.

Architecture

Hadrian's Gate resembles a typical Roman triumphal arch. Its three archways are of the same size - 4.15 meters wide and 6.18 meters in height, measured to the top of the arc. The whole structure has a height of more than 8 meters from the ancient pavement to the top of the entablature.

Both the front and the back side of the gate are adorned by the façades, composed of four columns each. The monument was built of white marble, with the exception of granite column shafts. The capitals of the columns are of the composite order, i.e. they combine the volutes of the Ionic order capital with the acanthus leaves of the Corinthian order.

The entablature above the colonnades extending on both sides of the gate has a height of 1.28 meters and consists of an architrave, a low frieze decorated with floral motifs and a cornice. The rich decoration of the cornice represents, among others, the heads of lions. The barrel vaults over the archways are decorated with caissons, each of which has a distinct decoration - floral motifs and rosettes.

Getting there:

Hadrian's Gate stands by the Atatürk Boulevard, in the centre of Antalya. It can be reached on foot, during a walk through by Kaleiçi historical district, or by tram. The tram line (called Nostalji tramvay) runs right by the monument, and the stop is called, fittingly, Hadrian.

Hıdırlık Tower in Antalya

Hıdırlık Tower (tr. Hıdırlık Kulesi) is one of these historical buildings, such as the Hadrian's Gate, the Fluted Minaret and the Clock Tower, which have become the symbols inextricably associated with Antalya. However, it is not really the tower itself that attracts many visitors, but the beautiful views of Antalya bay which looks especially stunning from this vantage point.

The tower is one of the oldest surviving monuments in the city. It is built of yellow-brown, stone blocks. Its lower story was erected on the square plan at the turn of the 2nd century AD as a part of the city fortifications. Soon, in the

2nd century, the second story was added, this time on the circular plan. The upper part of the building underwent extensive renovations during the Seljuk and Ottoman periods.

The function of this structure still remains a mystery. The popular belief is that the tower was actually the tomb of an important person. This hypothesis is confirmed by the fragments of frescoes preserved inside the building. Moreover, on both sides of the entrance gate there are stylized carvings of axes that could indicate the importance of the person buried in it.

On the other hand, the specific location of the tower - on top of a cliff near the port - can indicate another function of this structure. There is a belief that it used to be a lighthouse and a looked-out point from which the ships approaching Antalya were observed. Perhaps, for some time, the building was also used as a church.

The tower is 14 meters high. The entrance is located on the eastern side of the structure. It leads to a small room, from where a narrow staircase goes up to the top level. Currently, the main role of the tower is purely decorative. It is a popular place to come to just before the sunset, both for the tourists and the inhabitants of Antalya.

Getting there:

Hıdırlık Tower is located at the point where the historic Kaleiçi district borders a large Karaalioğlu park. It stands above the cliffs that rise south of the harbor which has been used since the Roman times. The tower's precise location is at the end of Hesapçı Sokak - a street that traverses the

Kaleiçi district and begins at the Hadrian's Gate. The distance between this Roman-period gate and Hıdırlık Tower is only 600 meters .

Planning a Trip in Antalya
Getting There
By Plane -- As the gateway to the "Turkish Riviera," Antalya's international airport is a destination for visitors on both direct and connecting flights from dozens and dozens of cities worldwide. In 2007, the city completed a second international terminal to accommodate the continued tourist growth of the region as a whole. Turkish Airlines (tel. 444-0849) and British Airways (tel. 0844/493-0787 in the U.K) inaugurated direct flights from London (Gatwick) to Antalya in June 2005 and April 2008, respectively. Pegasus Airlines and SunExpress (tel. 0232/444-0797 in Turkey) soon followed suit, flying from London's Stansted Airport (summers only). The U.K.-based charter Thomas Cook flies year-round from London Gatwick direct to Antalya.

Direct domestic service into Antalya from Istanbul is provided by Turkish Airlines from both Atatürk and Istanbul Sabiha Gökçen Airports (tel. 444-0849), Onur Air (tel. 0242/330-3432 in Antalya, or 0212/663-9176 in Istanbul), and Atlasjet (tel. 0216/444-3387). Pegasus and SunExpress also fly from Sabiha Gökçen Airport in Istanbul, while SunExpress also flies direct from Izmir and Bodrum. In summer, Fly Air (tel. 444-4359) resumes regular service to Antalya from Istanbul as well. (There are also direct flights from Adana, Trabzon, and Van, cities not covered in this guide.)

The airport is about 11km (6 3/4 miles) to the east of the city center on the main Antalya road/D400. If you're staying on Lara Beach, a taxi will be your best bet from the airport. If you're staying on Konyaalti Beach, take the Havas airport shuttle (tel. 444-0487 or 0242/312-2956; 10TL), which stops at the Sheraton Hotel on its way to the *otogar.* From the drop-off point, you can get a taxi to your final destination. For those whose final destination is Kaleiçi, get off the Havas bus at the Devlet Hastanesi (State Hospital). From there, it's but a few steps through the open air plaza to Cumhuriyhet Caddesi and the Clock Tower. From there, you can navigate on foot through the maze of the Old City to your hotel. Havas shuttle departures are scheduled to coincide with the arrival of domestic flights.

A taxi directly to/from the airport to the center of town costs around 30TL, more if your hotel is further afield. Nighttime rates are about 50% higher (many cities in Turkey are abolishing this nighttime rate to address the unfortunate fleecing of tourists who can't read the gündüz-day and gece-night indicators on the meter).

Major car rental companies with counters in the Domestic Terminal 1 are Avis (tel. 0242/330-3073; also downtown at Fevzi Çakmak Cad. 30, in the Divan Talya Hotel across from the Sheraton Voyager, tel. 0242/316-6148; open daily 9am-7pm), Budget (tel. 0242/330-3395), Europcar (tel. 0242/330-3068), Hertz (tel. 0242/330-3465), and National (tel. 0242/330-3557). National also has a presence in the International Terminal 2 (tel. 0242/330-3316).

By Bus -- Antalya is a major transport hub, with 167 bus companies and 633 minibuses serving a total of 147 routes. The major bus lines serving Antalya with frequent service are Varan, Ulusöy, Kamil Koç, Pamukkale, Uludag, and Boss. Sample fares are: from Istanbul (12 hr., 60TL), Izmir (7-8 hr., 35TL), and Denizli (3-4 1/2 hr., 20TL). For transport from the smaller towns along the coastline, you can hop on one of the frequent minibuses, Bati Antalya Tur is a good bet, arriving from Fethiye (21TL), Kalkan (15TL), Kas (13TL), and Demre (11TL), to name just a few.

The dual-terminal bus station lies 4km (2 1/2 miles) northwest of the town center on the highway to Burdur and is easily as user-friendly as the airport. A rail system that will eventually transport passengers from the bus station to the center of town and beyond is currently under development and should be completed by the second half of this century (optimistically). Otherwise, you'll have your choice between an excruciatingly slow municipal bus (located outside the minibus/*dolmus* terminal in front of the taxi stand, idling until its half-hourly departure; 1TL) or a taxi (cost to Kaleiçi: around 20TL to 25TL).

Visitor Information

The tourist information office (tel. 0242/241-1747) is about a 10-minute walk west of Kaleiçi down Cumhuriyet Caddesi, at Anafartalar Cad. 31. It's worth a visit for fliers and brochures on upcoming events. Or, save yourself a trip and pop into one of the many travel agencies lining the cobbled streets for the same information.

Orientation

The city of Antalya is built upon a limestone travertine formed from the springs that run down from the mountains, so that the city meets the sea by way of breathtaking cliffs. At the center is the cliff-top fortress neighborhood of Kaleiçi, full of elegant garden cafes and charming ramshackle eateries, all built atop pre-Roman, Roman, and Byzantine foundations. Kaleiçi, the hassling to get you to empty your wallet notwithstanding, is a charming area of restored Greek houses, Italian villas, and Ottoman Pasas' residences, some converted into guesthouses and hotels along narrow winding streets. At the base of the cliff is the harbor and marina, built over an ancient Roman harbor and now the center of the city's resort nightlife.

About a mile and a half to the west of Kaleiçi is Konyaalti, the pebbly beach beginning just west of the archaeological museum and extending (so far) for about 8km (5 miles). Development will continue up to the port, an extension that will simply put the icing on an already successful and crazily popular city/seaside resort destination. By day, beach umbrellas and lounges backed by cafes and green lawns are filled with sun-seekers; by night, the waterfront park gets strewn with oversize colored cushions and romantic lighting, and restaurant tables spill onto the beach park walkway.

To the east of Antalya center just past the cliffs is Lara Plaji, a long stretch of pebbly beach gives way to a long stretch of coarse sand coastline, and enough all-inclusive themed hotels (a replica of the Titanic, the Kremlin, and Venice, just to name a few) to earn the area the moniker "Las Vegas in Turkey." Still, at approximately 11km (6

3/4 miles) from Antalya city center, it's a bit of a stretch to recommend this beach, that is, unless combined with a jaunt to the Lower Düden Waterfalls.

Beyond the city limits, Antalya spreads out to the mountainous winding roads that meander along the Lycian Coast to the west, and to the all-inclusive resort hotels along the sandy beaches sprawled out to the east, past the haphazard, poured-concrete blocks typical of Turkish towns. Clear waters and sandy coastlines also lie at the base of Kaleiçi, at Memerli Plaji, and most archaeological sites and natural phenomena are within an hour of town.

Getting Around

The primarily pedestrian area in and around the old town of Kaleiçi (including the harbor) is very compact, and you'll have very little need to venture far from here if this is where you're holing up for the night. The tourist information office is at the Cliffside park just on the western fringes of Kaleiçi, while the archaeological museum is about a 20-minute walk to the west of the city center, also accessible by tramway.

From Kaleiçi to Konyaalti, it's about a 10TL unavoidably meandering taxi ride; it'll be cheaper on the way back because the one-way main avenue is now working in your favor.

By Tram -- An 8km (5-mile) tramway runs parallel to the coastline from the Antalya Museum to the neighborhoods east of Kaleiçi. Running every half-hour, it is particularly convenient as a way to get between Kaleiçi and the museum, Atatürk Parki, and Konyaalti Beach. There's a hop-on point on Cumhuriyet Caddesi across from the clock tower in Kaleiçi, and the fare is 1TL.

By Car -- A car in the region of Antalya is indispensable for a thorough exploration of the sights, sounds, and smells, but within the city itself, you may want to spend your energies doing something other than sitting in traffic and making sense of the one-way circuitous route through the center of town.

Although a car would be handy for a quick run to the museum, about a mile west of Kaleiçi, you'll be better off parking it and forgetting about it. The tram will take you practically door to door for 1TL and no hassle. For self-piloted day trips out of town, all major hotels have either on-site car rental or a concierge to help fix you up. Car rental companies abound in Kaleiçi, so your biggest challenge will be one of choice. A good bet is Gaye Rent a Car, Tuzcular Mah. Imaret Sok. 1, near the clock tower (tel. 0242/247-1000). Sample rates for a Honda Civic automatic is 60TL per day, including full insurance.

By Taxi -- Because Kaleiçi is a walking district, a taxi is mostly useful for getting back and forth between the marina/Kaleiçi and the museum (Konyaalti Beach, the Sheraton, and the Hillside Su are near the museum on the west side of town). Hiring a taxi is also an (albeit expensive) option for those unable or unwilling to rent wheels for day-tripping out of the city, but be sure to bargain (you will also pay for gas) because quoted rates are exorbitant. I recommend a tour to your nearby attraction of choice, at least for the professional guide and the camaraderie of your fellow visitors.

Fast Facts in Antalya

Airlines -- The local numbers for the main airlines are Domestic Terminal 1: Atlasjet (tel. 0242/330-3900), Fly Air (tel. 0242/330-3030), Turkish Airlines (tel. 0242/330-3230 or 444-0849), Pegasus (tel. 0242/330-3548), SunExpress (tel. 0242/310-2727 or 0232/444-0797); International Terminal 2: British Airways (tel. 0242/330-3969), Onur Air (tel. 0242/330-3371).

Airport -- For information on departures and arrivals call your airline direct. For general airport information, the number for Terminal 1 is tel. 0242/310-5500 Terminal 2 is tel. 0242/330-3600

Ambulance -- Call tel. 112.

Buses -- The main bus companies with a presence at Antalya's *otogar* are: Antalya Tur (tel. 0242/331-1084), Kamil Koç (tel. 0242/331-1170), Metro (tel. 0242/331-1050), Pamukkale (tel. 0242/332-1020), Ulusoy (tel. 0242/331-1310), and Varan (tel. 0242/331-1111).

Climate -- Antalya has four seasons: fall, winter, spring, and hell, when temperatures soar to digits even the government won't accurately report. (Everybody gets the day off when the mercury passes 104°F/40°C.) Humidity can sometimes reach into the triple digits as well.

Consulates -- The U.K. has a Vice Consulate at Fevzi Çakmak Cad. 1314, Sok. 6/8, Elif Apt. (tel. 0242/244-5313).

Festivals -- Antalya hosts the eminent Golden Orange Film Festival (tel. 0242/238-5444) in October. The Aspendos Theatre is reanimated under a moonlit sky in July, during the International Opera and Ballet Festival. For information on the festival schedule, tickets, or transportation, contact the Antalya Devlet Opera ve Balesi (tel. 0242/243-7640; fax 0242/243-8827). Additional events in and around Antalya are available through Antalya Festivals (tel. 0242/238-2776).

Hospitals -- The Antalya Anatolian Private Hospital (tel. 0242/249-3300) is at Çaybasi Mah. Burhanettin Onat Cad. 1352 Sok. You will also encounter English-speaking staff at the international Interhospital Antalya at Kiziltoprak Mah., Meydan PTT Arkasi (near the post office; tel. 0242/311-1500).

Laundry -- Bizim Çamasirhane does laundry for 10TL per load. It's located at Kiliçarslan Mah. Hesapçi Sok. Kesik Minare Yani 1 (tel. 0537/352-5782).

Post Office -- The main PTT is located at Anafartalar Caddesi, opposite the Turkish Airlines offices. It's open from 9am to 5pm for postal services and 24/7 for phone access.

Cuisine & restaurants

Cuisine of Antalya for gourmets. Places for dinner - best restaurants

The name of the restaurant Gizli Bahçe can be literally translated as "Secret Garden". It is located on one of the high cliffs, from which visitors can enjoy amazing panoramic views of the coast. The restaurant specializes in cooking dishes from the national cuisine, but its menu also contains delicacies from the international cuisine. In the evening in Gizli Bahçe plays live music and this place is always full of visitors. Blue

Parrot restaurant is a great place for family rest. In the morning the restaurant serves delicious English breakfast, afternoon is the time when visitors are welcome to enjoy various choice of salads and first courses, and in the evening don't hesitate to choose amazing delicacies. The restaurant often hosts engaging evening parties. From time to time huge plasma screens of the restaurant broadcast major sporting events, so Blue Parrot is loved not only by gourmets, but also by sports fans. When it comes to Chinese food restaurants, we should certainly mention China Garden, a part of the tables of which is served on a beautiful terrace. Beijing duck is considered the specialty of the restaurant. Fans of more original dishes will like soup with crab meat, as well as hot crackers made of shrimps with spicy chili sauce.

Fans of French cuisine will simply not find a better restaurant than Marina. Duck in orange sauce with walnuts, salmon roll with caviar and shrimps, seafood with signature saffron sauce these are just a few specialties that always keep the visitors of this restaurant fully delighted. When it is a dessert time, make your choice in favor of tender cakes the menu of the restaurant contains more than several dozen types of them. Stella's Bistro restaurant specializes in cooking Mediterranean food. Here you can try classic Italian lasagna, gentle pizza, as well as select from a large choice of sandwiches and salads. The restaurant's tables are located on a terrace, so while having their meal visitors can enjoy magnificent picturesque surroundings.

Kral Sofrasi restaurant is located not far away from marina. It will please lovers of Turkish cuisine. Among the most popular dishes of the restaurant is a huge casserole with meat and vegetables seasoned with chili sauce. It is simply impossible to ignore the restaurant named Sim, the menu of which will be appreciated by the followers of the vegetarian diet. The reason for this is in the restaurant's signature dish - stewed vegetables with spices. However, fans of meat delicacies will also find here several suitable dishes.

All ice cream fans should not forget to try Dondurma during their stay in Antalya. This popular dessert only looks like a classic ice cream as it is also served in crunchy cons. That said, the dessert tastes absolutely incredible and it is hard to compare it with anything else. Milk and sugar are the main ingredients of Dondurma, and that is why this dessert really resembles traditional ice cream. However, the dessert contains mastic and salep that make Dondurma quite viscous. Sometimes this dessert is so thick that one can eat it with fork and knife. Travelers will find this unusual specialty in many restaurants in Antalya. Numerous food carts also often sell Dondurma.

Travelers who cannot imagine their life without sweets will be pleasantly surprised with their stay in Antalya. Simply take a stroll to the city's markets that offer all kinds of the most popular pastries in the region. In addition to traditional Locum and Baklava that are familiar to many travelers, it is possible to try many other interesting sweet masterpieces.

Tulumba is a popular national pastry that is made of sweet dough. Tulumba can vary in shape and size. Sometimes it is cut into small sticks. Some chefs prefer to make gorgeous cracknels. It is better to eat this dessert when it is fresh because it slowly loses its original taste during the shelf life.

Pişmaniye is another popular dessert in Antalya that is sold in many cafes and food carts. The dessert resembles cotton candy, but it has more ingredients, such as pistachios, sesame seeds, and many other ingredients. Fans of halva should head to the district of Kaleiçi in Antalya as chefs in this part of the city cook this dessert in accordance with ancient recipes.

Fans of pastries will enjoy traditional buns with sesame that are very popular in Antalya. Travelers will find vendors selling these buns virtually everywhere. Popular buns are delicious and inexpensive. In order to get acquainted with the culinary traditions of Antalya, travelers do not necessarily need to attend expensive restaurants. It is possible to try unique food right on the city's streets and markets.

Traditions & lifestyle

Colors of Antalya - traditions, festivals, mentality and lifestyle

Local residents follow a large number of religious traditions and customs. Despite the fact that women now have equal rights with men, they still have to stick to some ancient traditions. For example, they cannot go out without a special headscarf just like centuries ago, and clothes must remain closed and spacious. The indigenous people are quite tolerant to the traditions of travellers, but visitors are encouraged to follow some of the local customs. You shouldn't make a walk wearing provoking clothes, do not drink alcoholic beverages in the wrong places and do not forget to take off your shoes at the entrance to someone's house.

It is worth noting that the locals are very friendly, polite and hospitable. When communicating with new friends they pay attention, first of all, to manners of a newcomer and how good a person is familiar with the rules of the etiquette. Travelers are strongly recommended to learn at least several phrases in Turkish prior a trip to Turkey. Just a few phrases in their native language can make the locals very friendly, and they will be happy to help a polite tourist who is interested in their national culture. As a rule, every house always serves a table for guests, so coming to a house of a local resident suddenly is simply impossible. Tables for guests always contain fruits and sweets; hospitable hosts only need to make a coffee and dishes for guests will be completely ready.

Many travellers even consider the hospitality of the locals a bit intrusive. Sellers in the stores will definitely try to invite a passerby to come in for a cup of coffee. While guests enjoy the flavorful drink, sellers will tell them about the most interesting products and provide recommendations concerning best restaurants and shopping centers of the city. If tourists refuse to accept such invitation, it can seriously offend a host, so make sure your pay a little attention to a generous merchant and do not forget to thank him for his warm welcome.

An orange has become a kind of a local peculiarity and the national symbol of the city. Monuments with a picture of the fruit can be seen right at every step in the city. The monuments of the fruit found in the city are made of different materials - stone, wood and plastic. Even entrances to some of the cafes and markets are decorated with colorful posters with the image of an orange. Throughout a year the residents of Antalya celebrate a series of interesting events, but the majority of them are connected to the lunar calendar, so these holidays do not have an exact binding to a particular date.

In May, the guests of the resort and local people will visit the Antalya Flower Festival. This event is considered one of the most colorful and impressive in Turkey. Local residents of Antalya plant extraordinary flowers with great love and every year they improve their skills. The annual Flower Festival is the real opportunity for them to show the miracles of gardening and demonstrate the achievements in flower breeding to numerous tourists. The festival is always held in May when Antalya turns into a fairytale flower city. During the event, you will see the flower platforms, moving slowly along the streets of the city, with wonderful floral figures. The flower festival is of great importance for the life of the country, it's like, another visit card of Turkey, which is proved by the presence of top management and officials of Antalya at the festival. The festival of flowers is not only a festive procession but also a lot of interesting festive events, such as exhibitions and competitions of flower decorators, fairs, and shows.

In June you will have a great chance to witness Antalya Opera and Ballet Festival. Music fans can attend the Antalya Jazz Festival, as well as Abdal

Musa festival, and Fenike festival in Antalya. July is the time for an exciting Antalya Tourism Festival. Holidaymakers who planned their trip to August will attend the Antalya International Festival of Folk Music and Dance. This event gathers creative bands from all over the world and local choirs, orchestras, theater groups, and children teams, who perform in different genres. The main rule is that it should not be boring. Another condition organizers of the festival require from the participants is the involvement of spectators in the show. Tourists will be offered to study national songs, dance and perform together with artists. The main concert of the festival is held in the evening and lasts until late night. In September, the resort city invites tourists and their fellow travelers the

Ibradi grape festival and the Golden Orange film festival.

Golden Orange is the important film festival in Turkey and one of the most respected in Asia. The first festival was held in 1964, and its first aim was to support Turkish cinema. In the main program of the festival participate more than one hundred films of different genres. This movie festival is not only a cultural event, but also a social one, during which you can visit various meetings with famous actors, cinematographers, concerts, and parties. In Antalya, on the beach of Lara, the festival of sand sculptures takes place. Sandland is the mega-exhibition: 10 thousand tons of sand on an area of 10 thousand square meters will be turned into unique sculptures by hands of artists who come here from around the world. Visitors are allowed to show their creative abilities: a special area is allocated on the territory, where everyone can make a small masterpiece if desired. In October, the International Mediterranean Music Festival starts on the Turkish coast.

Where to stay?

Extraordinary hotels
Extraordinary hotels - best choice for your unusual city break in Antalya
The Marmara Antalya
From Antalya center - 4.4 km
Some hotels of Antalya are unique, and all thanks to superb infrastructure, special design and services. The main feature of The Marmara Antalya hotel is a huge rotating lobby, where guests can enjoy views of the surrounding area while tasting exquisite treats and cocktails.

Besides the luxurious lobby and stylish rooms, the hotel can boast the famous organic restaurant Marmara Tuti. It has a special menu; all dishes are cooked exclusively of local organic products.

Hotel SU
From Antalya center - 3.9 km
Luxury Hotel SU is designed in unique style. Artistic lighting in the rooms and in public areas is a hallmark of the place. The lounge decorated in white tones stands out among other premises. Thanks to huge spherical chandeliers this club-style lounge shines with thousands of bright sparks making the atmosphere fantastic. Small fixtures are mounted in the furniture and walls of the hotel, thanks to which elegant rooms with panoramic windows shine with all the colors of the rainbow.

Atelya Art Hotel
From Antalya center - 0.3 km
Tourists would be impressed not only by the luxury hotels in Antalya, but also with modest budget places, including Atelya Art Hotel . This hotel is set in a historic building that is a real historic landmark. In the courtyard, guests can see the old marble well, which for many years has being the main source of water for the home owners. The picturesque courtyard has a cozy sitting area with a pool and a bar, where you can taste popular national food. The hotel is full of national charm. It features a rich collection of works of art; everywhere you can see luxurious fabrics and handmade rugs.

Hadrianus Hotel
From Antalya center - 0.4 km
The main feature of Hadrianus Hotel is incomparable interior designed in the Ottoman

style. The old building has 10 rooms, each of which is unique and affects with abundance of themed accessories. Chic fabric with golden embroidery, amazing wall panels of dark wood, rich carpets and antique furniture decorate all the rooms. Some rooms even provide plush bathrobes with hand-embroidery in the style of yesteryear. In addition to the unique ambience, the hotel can boast chic orchard. Some mighty trees have been planted there over a hundred years ago.

Antalya Farm House
From Antalya center - 12.3 km
Antalya Farm House is very popular among travelers with children; it's considered the best hotel for nature lovers. This wonderful hotel&farm can be found in a lush garden. This place takes travelers with pets. There are various animals kept onsite, so guests will have an

opportunity to watch the geese and turtles, as well as enjoy relaxed family atmosphere. The hotel has a large garden growing vegetables used for cooking in the restaurant. Vacationers can pick oranges and peaches just off braches. The garden is equipped with a lot of amazing places to rest and play with children.

Stylish design-hotels

Stylish weekend in Antalya collection of top unique boutique hotels
Antalya doesn't experience a lack of designer hotels. The incredibly stylish and attractive accommodation place is Prime Boutique Hotel. It's set in an elegant building with white facade. The hotel offers customers bright rooms with full-size picture windows. Cream shades dominate in design and go well with fabrics of saturated colors. All rooms are elegantly

furnished in the style of past years. Suites have a huge bed in colonial style with a lovely four-poster bed dressed in linen of natural fabrics.

Elegance East Hotel
From Antalya center - 0.5 km
Elegance East Hotel offers travelers to spend a few days in the unique atmosphere of yesteryear. Interior of this elegant and romantic hotel is a wonderful combination of old traditions and contemporary style. Luxury curtains with patterns on the windows, lovely upholstered ottomans, huge old-style chandeliers, large beds with high carved back and mirrors in gilt frame make ambience of rooms very harmonious. There are also some modern design elements, including paintings in contemporary style, cabinets with glass sliding doors and elegant parquet floor.

A complex of two restored mansions is occupied by Kauçuk Residence. It also differs with amazing interior. Each of its rooms is special; some have saved pristine stone walls and beamed ceilings, while others boast unique antique furniture. There are also romantic rooms with a carved wooden ceiling and a crystal chandelier in yesteryear style, as well as a very nice drapery of light-colored fabrics. Mansions are surrounded by picturesque tropical garden with landscaped terraces.

Otantik Hotel
From Antalya center - 0.3 km
If you want to spend a few days in atmosphere of unique national colour, then visit Otantik Hotel . It occupies an elegant building in the Ottoman style decorated in accordance with the brightest local traditions. The hotel has an amazing finish of dark wood. Authentic brass

luminaires and lamps, satin of saturated colors and crafts by local artisans complement the interior scene. The courtyard of the hotel has a wonderful terrace decorated with plants in nice clay pots and vases.

La Boutique Antalya
From Antalya center - 5.3 km
La Boutique Antalya hotel is designed in unique style. This accommodation place is situated on the cliffs of Falaise and occupies an elegant building in the style of yesteryear. There are luxurious rooms with sliding full-size picture windows; all rooms are brightly furnished in Art Deco style. Decorations include luxurious satin and velvet, as well as gilded ornaments. Design of the hotel's territory also deserves special attention. In addition to a spacious terrace and deck chairs you can find huge white tents with cushioned furniture.

Frankfurt Hotel
From Antalya center - 0.3 km
Amazing atmosphere is the hallmark of the modest budget Frankfurt Hotel . It was opened in a renovated historic building. Interior of the hotel is based on finishing of precious wood and wooden furniture, many pieces of which are made by hand. Decorations include unique paintings and copper accessories in traditional style. The hotel can boast a patio. It's literally immersed in lush flowers and greenery; vines come down the walls of the building and form amazing landscape compositions.

Hotels with history

Preserved history of Antalya: long-standing and historical hotels
Mediterra Art Hotel
From Antalya center - 0.3 km

Antalya has wonderful hotels that keep the atmosphere of bygone times, and the picturesque Mediterra Art Hotel is among them. The luxury Ottoman-style building housing the hotel has retained a number of old-style pieces. It features restored finishing of wood and stone, and some fragments of walls are hand-painted. Antique furniture and bright accessories in traditional style, including smart fixtures, wall panels and paintings, complement the interior scene. The unique Mediterra art gallery, which represents the most famous paintings by local artists, can be found onsite.

Minyon Hotel
From Antalya center - 0.5 km
Minyon Hotel is situated in the picturesque historic district of Kaleici. Its spectacular building in the traditional style is one of the prominent historical attractions of Antalya. The hotel is

striking with historic luxury. There are pristine stone walls and wooden ceilings. Everywhere you can see gorgeous wooden furniture, rich carpets and brass fixtures. The ground floor of the hotel has an amazing recreation area boasting a collection of clay pots and old paintings.

Tuvana Hotel
From Antalya center - 0.1 km
Guests of Tuvana Hotel will be able to live in unique atmosphere of past centuries. The hotel occupies a complex of four luxurious stone buildings surrounded by lush tropical garden and separated by cobbled alleys. The ambience in the mansions isn't inferior to the rich modern museums, as each element of the decor can be safely called a priceless exhibit. Antique furniture upholstered in colorful fabrics, impressive crystal

chandeliers and an interesting collection of paintings deserve special attention.

Romantic Ottoman Suites Hotel is designed In accordance with traditions of past years. It occupies a renovated historic building in the center of the resort and offers guests a choice of 12 rooms with individual design. All rooms come with luxurious parquet floor and lovely wallpaper with floral motifs. Wooden furniture upholstered in exquisite fabrics of pearly shades creates special ambience. Thanks to the huge gilded mirrors and chandeliers rooms seem incredibly spacious and bright.

Alp Pasa Hotel
From Antalya center - 0.3 km
Vacations at Alp Pasa Hotel promise to be memorable. Here rooms are designed in different styles, and there are lots of places for

recreation. The national restaurant occupies an old hall with vaulted ceiling. The courtyard boasts a lovely pool and several spacious terraces. Guests of the hotel will be able to choose a room that has a huge wooden four-poster bed. Some suites feature pristine stone walls and huge wrought iron chandeliers in medieval style.

Agatha Lodge & More located a few minutes' walk from Mermerli Beach enjoys popularity among fans of unusual accommodation places. Its main feature is incomparable interior made in full accordance with traditions of past years. All furniture is made exclusively of natural wood and decorated with intricate carvings; elegant beds are covered with a coverlet featuring bright patterns. Absolutely all rooms have paintings by local artists. Here and there you could find old stone niches that are used to store amazing craft works.

Luxury accommodation
Top places to stay in Antalya most luxury and fashionable hotels
Ramada Plaza Antalya
From Antalya center - 1.1 km
Antalya is the perfect place for upscale vacations, which will be even more amazing, if you choose the right hotel. One of the most luxurious places is Ramada Plaza Antalya resort situated on the picturesque coast, a few minutes' walk from Kaleici. The main feature of the hotel is a large-scale City Club spa that offers various types of massage, Turkish bath, sauna and many other services. The hotel has spacious and romantic suites on the upper floors. They feature huge panoramic windows with views of the coast.

Rixos Downtown
From Antalya center - 2.7 km

The luxurious hotel Rixos Downtown won't disappoint experienced travelers. It attracts customers with its impeccable infrastructure and first-class service. The hotel is set a high-rise building surrounded by landscaped gardens. Its vast grounds are equipped with a variety of nice pools, gazebos and cozy terraces. Guests can choose from 4 different restaurants and bars. The upper floors of the hotel feature gorgeous suites with full-size picture windows.

Harrington Park Resort
From Antalya center - 7 km

One of the best hotels in Antalya is Harrington Park Resort . It has more than 300 rooms of different classes, among which there are luxurious suites with a private terrace decorated in cream colors. Connoisseurs of luxury can be accommodated in the presidential suite of 225 m2. Accommodation there will cost more than 1,000 USD per night. The suite is decorated in shades of coffee, it has a beautiful bathroom with a jacuzzi and dark wood trim. Guests can get to the furnished terrace right out of the bathroom. The former is furnished with white chairs; it's securely hidden from prying eyes.

Crowne Plaza Antalya
From Antalya center - 7.3 km
It's certainly worth noting Crowne Plaza Antalya among the most prestigious hotels in Antalya. It occupies a nice building in the traditional style and has romantic atmosphere. Couples will be able to stay in one of the exclusive rooms. The main feature of these rooms is a large marble-furnished bathroom with a panoramic window and a hot tub.

An elegant building with a glass facade houses Oz Hotels Antalya Hotel Resort & Spa. It will appeal to those who like to rest at resorts and enjoy spa treatments. Apart from the traditional Turkish bath, the spa boasts a fully equipped fitness center with cardiovascular machines and a variety of beauty parlors. Those who wish to arrange a celebration at the hotel could use a very unusual banquet room with a vaulted ceiling decorated with pearl-colored fabrics. Gourmets will enjoy the on-site restaurant, where they can taste branded dishes of seafood.

Porto Bello Hotel Resort & Spa is ready to please everyone without exception. Its upscale amenities deserve special attention. The place has both rooms suitable for a large company and suites for fans of exclusive rest. Luxury suites of 50m2 differ with sophisticated finish of rare wood and marble. There are also beamed ceiling in the style of the past and exquisite carpets of saturated blue shade.

Romantic hotel

Antalya for couples in love best hotels for intimate escape, wedding or honeymoon
Ninova Pension
From Antalya center - 0.3 km
Antalya has lots of incredibly romantic hotels, rest in which will be unforgettable. Modest hotel Ninova Pension is full of charm; it's perfect for thrifty travelers. It has wonderful rooms for couples, with a big bed with carved back; beds are usually dressed in linen of delicate pink color. Guests can stroll through the picturesque orchard or arrange a romantic dinner and taste popular national food from the restaurant at one of the furnished terraces.

Hotel Oscar
From Antalya center - 0.6 km
The lovely Hotel Oscar is popular among couples. In addition to comfortable rooms it offers a lot of great entertainment options. The hotel has two wonderful bars, one of which features a large outdoor pool, and the other has an incredibly cozy room with a fireplace. You can taste exotic cocktails there or order a hookah. The onsite restaurant is perfect for arranging a celebration. In clear weather its tables are served in the garden.

Bilem High Class Hotel
From Antalya center - 4.8 km
Those preferring to have first-class vacations are recommended to stay at Bilem High Class Hotel . It's literally immersed in romantic atmosphere. Spacious rooms are designed in cream colors and decorated with aristocratic gold accessories.

Some suites have an exclusive open bathroom with a jacuzzi. A chic restaurant decorated with crystal chandeliers can enchant the discerning visitor. It serves classic national food and fine wines imported from various countries of the world. Guests can relax after a busy day at the spa, where various massages are offered.

Villa Verde
From Antalya center - 0.4 km
Couples will have an opportunity to spend vacations in unique atmosphere of past centuries. Villa Verde set in a beautiful Ottoman villa is equipped in accordance with traditions of the past. In addition to the standard rooms, the hotel has a chic double suite featuring a huge wooden bed with a translucent canopy. Superb finish of natural wood makes rooms even more intimate. Public areas are decorated with works of art and crafts in the national style. The hotel is

surrounded with lush garden of 280m2, which will be the best place for an evening stroll.

Deja Vu Hotel
From Antalya center - 0.2 km
Family Deja Vu Hotel located in the historic district of Antalya offers to rest in casual atmosphere. Everyone will feel as a welcome guest in this picturesque hotel; it will fit couples of all ages. Its interior is full of antique ornaments. The garden is equipped with a gorgeous pool and plenty of lovely terraces. By nightfall, hotel's grounds are illuminated with artistic lighting, which makes the ambience even more romantic.

Seven Stars Exclusive Hotel
From Antalya center - 7 km
Seven Stars Exclusive Hotel offers exclusive vacations for couples. It occupies a very nice building resembling an old Ottoman tower.

Rooms are decorated in contemporary style complemented by colorful modern paintings. The patio has an elegant seating area with a pool, a bar and landscaped gardens. Upon arrival of the guests rooms are always decorated with beautiful decorative candles and rose petals. Customers can arrange a celebration in a stylish restaurant with panoramic windows.

Shopping in Antalya

Shopping in Antalya - authentic goods, best outlets, malls and boutiques
One of the most popular shopping centers in Antalya is ATM Deepo Outlet. This is a huge outlet, where you can buy quality brand clothes throughout the year on special offer. Despite the lowest possible price level, all goods are of decent quality. They offer nice casual clothes, shoes for every taste, sportswear and beach

accessories. Ladies will definitely enjoy a wide choice of dresses. There are also several large shops with goods for children.

No less popular is Migros shopping center whose opening took place in 2001. This is a large trading and entertainment complex, where you can do some shopping and have a good time with your whole family. The complex is full of clothing and footwear stores of every price category. Here, you will find budget brands and interesting designer things. A store of the popular Turkish LC Waikiki brand is also here. It sells men's, women's and children's clothes. All the products presented are of decent quality, prices will definitely please frugal buyers. In addition to clothing, you can buy cosmetics and perfumes and then take a break in a movie or in one of the nearby cozy restaurants.

Women who want to bring organic cosmetics from Antalya should visit one of Watsons store. These stores offer customers essential oils and oil-based cosmetics. Shops of the network are represented in all major shopping centers of the city. You can purchase luxury creams, handmade soaps, perfumes based on essential oils and other interesting cosmetics, the like of which you won't find in European stores.

One of the biggest in Antalya is TerraCity trading complex. It has more than 160 shops, representing clothes and shoes of popular European and Turkish brands. There is even a large electronics store that offer new gadgets at much lower prices than in Europe. This place will be of interest to holidaymakers with children. It houses a large Burberry & Burberry Kids children's clothing store. Kids will be charmed with lots of attractions.

If the products presented in these stores are not enough, you can look into MarkAntalya trading complex. You can buy literally everything here from fashionable clothes of popular brands to local products and original souvenirs. There are some large cosmetics and perfumery shops and more than ten restaurants and cafes for visitors.

For the most beautiful souvenirs in national style, go to Lidya Suzani Carpet Gallery. They sell chic carpets, handkerchiefs and shawls. Here, you can choose cute pads with embroidery in oriental style as well as hand-sewn fabrics. All the products presented here are of the highest quality.

Many tourists prefer Kundu bazaar shopping center, where you can find not only pavilions with clothes and shoes, but plenty of nice souvenir shops. Here, you can choose smart glasses for walking along the coast, purchase electronics, popular national products and essential goods.

Antalya Market is necessarily worth noting. A walk across it promises to be an unforgettable event. Hundreds of shopping tents with clothes, souvenirs, spices, bright carpets and national costumes - you can buy literally everything here. They sell spices and popular national sweets as well as local cosmetics based on organic components. The market offers a wide choice of fresh fruits and vegetables. Prices are certainly higher than in many shopping centers but you definitely have to bargain with sellers.

Tips for tourists

Preparing your trip to Antalya: advices & hints - things to do and to obey

1. Fans of beach rest are better to visit Antalya during the period from April to October during this time of a year prevails a clear sunny weather. Those, who expect spending more time on trips, are better not to travel to the city during summer hot weather can break your plans.

2. Do not make photos of the local people on the streets, especially women dressed in black shawls this is forbidden. Before you take a picture of a man, make sure you ask him for permission.

3. Entering houses and mosques can be made only after you remove your shoes. Make sure you are quiet in the mosque. Do not forget to

pay your attention to your outfit before you plan to visit a mosque. Tourists wearing revealing or bright clothes may be simply rejected to enter the territory of many places of interest.

4. Drinking alcoholic beverages on the streets of the city is forbidden. Alcohol can be even removed from the menus of many restaurants during important religious celebrations.

5. Do not forget to leave tips in restaurants and cafes of the city. An average sum of tips is about 5 - 10% of the total bill. Porters and maids in hotels should also receive their small rewards.

6. Do not forget to bargain in local markets and in retail stores. For local merchants bargaining has become a kind of a ritual. Asking for a discount is not appropriate, probably, in large supermarkets only. When you go to a market, it

is better to take a lot of money in small denominations, so it will be easier to pay to sellers. Many of them can simply pretend that they do not have the change, thus increasing the price of a product.

7. Clothing and jewelry are better to buy in special shops. The quality of jewelry in street markets can be quite doubtful.

8. The majority of attractions are easily accessible by buses, but tourists usually prefer to use the services of taxis. You can catch a free car literally on any street of the city. We recommend discussing the price of a ride in advance because not all drivers have counters in their cars.

9. The best way to get water for drinking is to buy it in shops. Drinking tap water may affect your health not in the best way.

The End

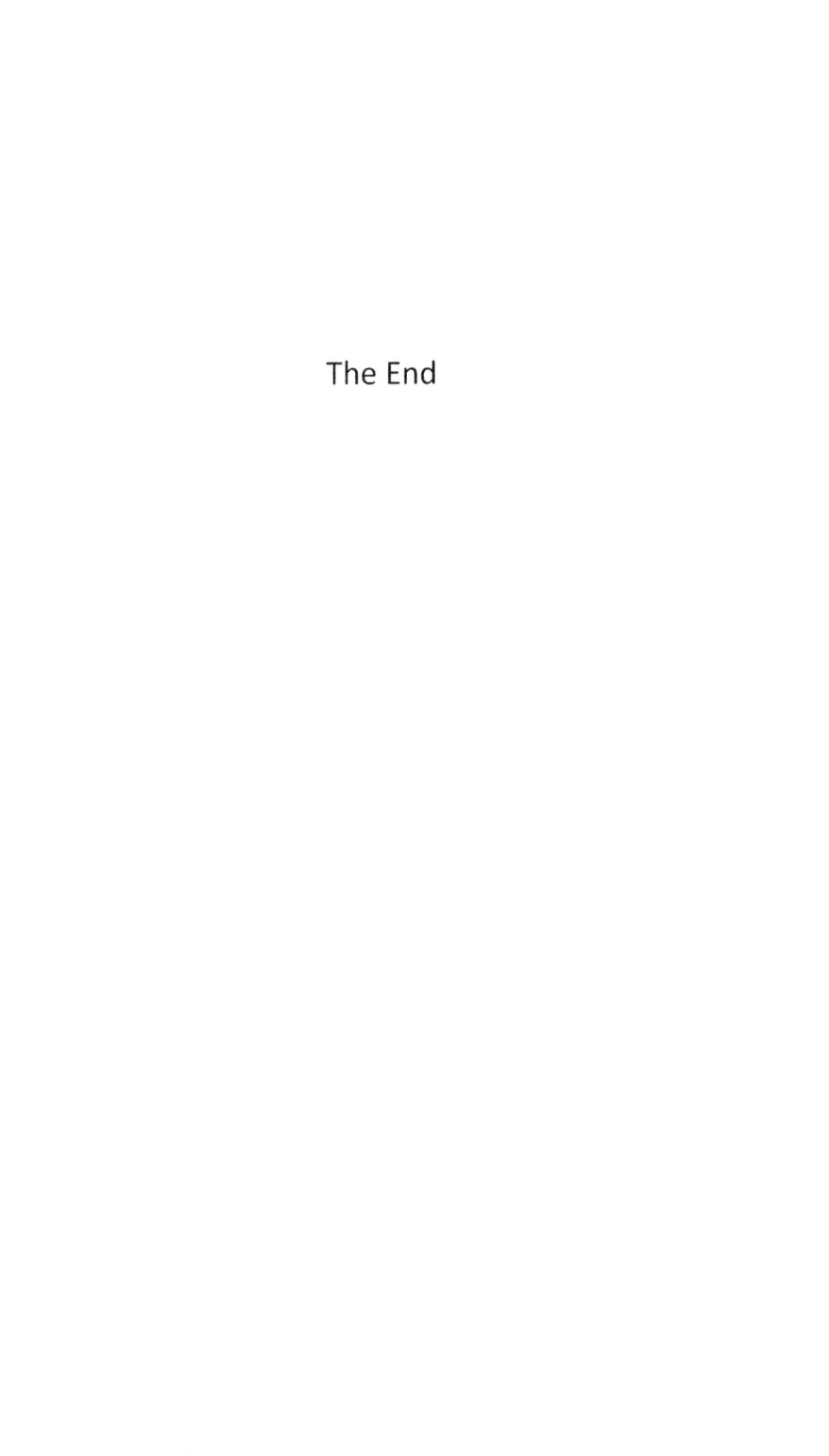

Printed in Great Britain
by Amazon